# The Origin and Meaning
## of Hasidism

# The Origin and Meaning of Hasidism

### MARTIN BUBER

*Edited and Translated by*
*Maurice Friedman*

.

HORIZON PRESS       NEW YORK

Copyright © 1960 by Martin Buber
Library of Congress Catalog Card No. 60-8161
ISBN 0-8180-1316-8 (cloth), 0-8180-1315-x (paper)
Manufactured in the United States of America

# CONTENTS

# EDITOR'S INTRODUCTION

In *The Origin and Meaning of Hasidism* Martin Buber completes his great lifework of the re-creation and interpretation of Hasidism, the popular communal mysticism that arose and flourished among the Jews of Eastern Europe in the eighteenth and nineteenth centuries. One of the greatest contemporary philosophers and a revolutionary influence on contemporary theology, Martin Buber has shown once again in this volume that the God of the Bible and of Hasidism is the loving God whose love includes the demand that man make real his humanity through bringing every aspect of his life into his relation to God.

Professor Buber's work is less concerned with defining theoretical concepts than with pointing to an image of man, a way of life. "He who expects of me a teaching other than a pointing of this character will always be disappointed," writes Buber. Nowhere is this "pointing" clearer than in his fifty-five-year work of re-creating the tales and teachings of the Hasidim. The theoretical doctrines of Hasidism are only a commentary on the Hasidic mode of life, says Buber in the present volume. "Our chief source of knowledge of Hasidism is its legends." These he has retold and commented on in many works; yet it has also been necessary for him to make explicit the place of Hasidism among world religions and its significance for the modern world. This is the task which he has accomplished in the present volume. Throughout a long lifetime Buber has been convinced that Hasidism, more than any other teaching, has the power to remind modern man of what he is in danger of forgetting—"for what purpose we are on earth." Although Buber is one of the greatest scholars of Hasidism, his concern with it has not been merely an academic one. If he has "carried it into the world against its will," as he says in the Foreword to this volume, it is not for the sake of its cultural interest or even its contribution as an example of a genuinely Jewish mysticism, but "because of its truth and because of the great need of the hour."

*The Origin and Meaning of Hasidism* is the second volume of Martin Buber's two-volume comprehensive interpretation, *Hasidism and the Way of Man*. The more illustrative first volume—*Hasidism and Modern Man* (Horizon Press, 1958)—is here completed by a group of interpretative essays written over a period of thirty years. The first three essays—"The Beginnings," "The Foundation Stone," and "Spinoza, Sabbatai Zvi, and the Baal-Shem"—deal with the life and teaching of the founder of Hasidism, Israel ben Eliezer, the Good Master of the Name of God (Baal-Shem-Tov). They bring out the significance of the Baal-Shem's teaching

for his time and ours by contrasting it with two contemporary doctrines—the philosophy of Spinoza and
Sabbatianism, the devastating Jewish gnostic and
pseudo-Messianic movement of the seventeenth
and eighteenth centuries. At the same time, they reach
back to the origins of Hasidism in the Kabbala (the esoteric "tradition" of Jewish-mysticism) and forward to a
comparison and contrast between the Hasidic image of
"raising the sparks" and the Freudian concept of sublimation. The fourth essay, "Spirit and Body of the
Hasidic Movement," presents the circles of the crowd
seeking help, of the Hasidic community, and of the
disciples, and, at the center of these circles, the zaddik, or rebbe, the leader of the Hasidic community.
The fifth, "Symbolic and Sacramental Existence," sets
Hasidism in the broad context of sacramental existence
in all times and religions. It shows, in particular, the
essential continuity between Hasidism and Biblical
prophecy. The sixth, "God and the Soul," distinguishes
Hasidism as a "mysticism become ethos" from the mysticism of Sankara and Meister Eckhart, two great rep-
resentatives of Hindu and Christian mysticism, and
shows the link between the Biblical Creator, the "Absolute Person" implicit in the Hasidic concept of
*tsimtsum,* and the "Eternal Thou" of Buber's own
"I-Thou" philosophy of religion. The seventh essay,
"Redemption," links the redemption of the Shekina,
God's indwelling Glory, with the redemption of Israel
through the return of the people to the land of Palestine. The fervent "Zionism" of the early Hasidim, the
burning desire of the great Hasidic leaders and many

of their followers to "go up to the Land," never meant that they aimed at making Israel a nation "like all the other nations" or an end in itself. "Hasidism is a great revelation of spirit and life in which the nation appears to be connected by an inner tie with the world, with the soul, and with God," writes Buber in this essay. "Only through such a contact," he concludes, "will it be possible to guard Zionism against following the way of the nationalism of our age, which, by demolishing the bridges which connect it with the world, is destroying its own value and its right to exist."

The eighth essay, "The Place of Hasidism in the History of Religion," is of particular interest to the American reader because of its sensitive comparison between Hasidism and a surprisingly similar movement sprung from utterly different roots—Zen Buddhism. Largely through the work of Daisetz T. Suzuki, Zen Buddhism has attracted ever-increasing attention in American intellectual and cultural circles in the last few years. Though more purely a scholar and less a re-creator than Buber, Suzuki in his lifework as interpreter of Zen to the Western world is strikingly similar to Buber in his lifelong task as interpreter of Hasidism. What makes this essay of Buber's a unique contribution to comparative religion, however, is not merely the fact that it brings out unsuspected resemblances between two movements each of which by itself is of great current interest. It also makes faithful distinctions in context and in spirit where these must be made, shows the divergences even within basic similarities, yet avoids at every point the oversimple contrasts between Eastern and Western, mystical and nonmystical, theistic and a-theistic religions that the current popularizers of Zen so easily fall into. Buber's conclusion, in fact, is a challenge to one of the most common distinctions among historians of religion and theologians, namely, that of the essential incompatibility between religions of inner illumination and religions of revelation. Hasidism is unique in that it is "the only mysticism in which *time* is hallowed." Because of its simultaneous concern for historical tradition and the living present, Hasidism explodes the familiar view of mysticism that sets it in contrast with faith. "Mysticism is the sphere on the borderland of faith," writes Buber, "in which the soul draws breath between word and word."

The Supplement, "Christ, Hasidism, Gnosis," demands a special word of explanation. It cannot stand by itself as a separate essay since it is a reply to an extended criticism of Buber's interpretation of Hasidism by Rudolf Pannwitz, a well-known German writer. Yet following the precedent of Buber's *Eclipse of God,* where we included as a supplement Buber's reply to a critique by C. G. Jung, I feel it justified here too to print Buber's rejoinder, taken out of its polemical context, for the sake of the clarification which it gives to important aspects of his thought.

Buber's juxtaposition of Hasidism, Christianity, and gnosis in this essay is by no means accidental, for the contrast between Hasidism and gnosis, and the comparison and contrast between Hasidism and Christianity, is implicit or explicit in most of Buber's essays on Hasidism. Since his early writings, Buber has seen important resemblances between Hasidism and the teachings of Jesus, and in *Two Types of Faith,* his study of Jesus and Paul, Buber compares Jesus's protest against action without inner intention and his teaching of love for the enemy with the Hasidic attitude on the same subjects. Yet Buber also sees a difference between the Christianity which sees in Jesus the Christ, the Messiah Come, and Hasidism, which preserves the Messianic tension in its concern for hallowing the everyday but leaves its "suffering servants" hidden in the "shadow of the quiver" waiting in each generation anew for God's hand to draw them forth and shoot them when he will. "Christ, Hasidism, Gnosis" is particularly helpful in this connection as a supplement to "Spinoza, Sabbatai Zvi, and the Baal-Shem." In its contrast between the *devotio* of Hasidism and the gnosis of Gnosticism and the Kabbala, it also serves as a supplement to Buber's treatment of Sabbatianism and Jacob Frank in the first two essays and of the Kabbala in "Symbolic and Sacramental Existence." "Where the mystic vortex circled, now stretches the way of man," Buber concludes "Christ, Hasidism, Gnosis." "In Hasidism *devotio* has absorbed and overcome gnosis. This must happen ever again if the bridge over the chasm of being is not to fall in."

In both supplements, the reply to Rudolf Pannwitz in this volume and the reply to Carl Jung in *Eclipse of God,* Buber is centrally concerned with the modern manifestation of gnosis, or Gnosticism, that age-old strain, held in suspension within many religions and philosophies and crystallized out in many movements and sects, which emphasizes a secret knowledge that delivers the man who knows from a dark and evil world in which he is essentially not at home, a knowledge which is itself salvation for the knower. Buber's rejection of gnosis must be understood within the context of the central attitude which unites his interpretation of Hasidism, his interpretation of Biblical Judaism, and his dialogical philosophy of religion—"holy insecurity." "Holy insecurity" is life lived in the Face of God. It is the very opposite of any security of salvation. The prophets of Israel, writes Buber, "always aimed to shatter all security and to proclaim in the opened abyss of the final insecurity the unwished-for God who demands that His human creatures become real . . . and confounds all who imagine that they can take refuge in the certainty that the temple of God is in their midst." The key to this "holy insecurity" is the "ever-anew" of each situation as opposed to the "once-for-all" with which man tries to abstract himself from the concrete. The meeting with God takes place in the "lived concrete," writes Buber, and lived concreteness exists only in so far as the moment retains its true dialogical character of presentness and uniqueness.

There are many types of "once-for-all," but all have in common the fact that they make unnecessary real response to the unique situation that confronts one in each hour. The logical God of the theologians—the God who can be put into a system or enclosed in an idea—is not the God who can be met in the lived concrete. The "once-for-all" of dogma resists the unforeseeable moment in similar fashion and thereby becomes "the most exalted form of invulnerability against revelation." From dogma it is only a step in the one direction to magic and in the other to gnosis, the two aspects of the Kabbala against which, according to Buber, Hasidism protests. A God that can be fixed in dogma can also be possessed and used. Magic operates wherever one celebrates "without being turned to the Thou and . . . really meaning its Presence." In magic God becomes a bundle of powers, present at a man's command and in the form in which man wishes them.

"Gnosis," says Buber, is the attempt to raise the veil which divides the revealed from the hidden and to lead forth the divine mystery. Gnosis, like magic, stands as the great threat to the life of dialogue and to the turning to God. Gnosis attempts to see through the contradiction of existence and free itself from it, rather than endure the contradiction and redeem it. In his comparison between Hasidism and the Kabbala in "Symbolic and Sacramental Existence" Buber sets forth in the sharpest terms the contrast between the security of gnosis and the "holy insecurity" of *devotio*. This gnosis is found not only in the Kabbala and in ancient gnostic sects but in some of the most active strains of modern culture. It is most obvious in theosophies and occult systems, but it is no less powerful and pervasive in other forms. In many theologies "unveiling gestures are to be discovered behind the interpreting ones," and gnosis has even found its way into modern psychotherapy:

> The psychological doctrine which deals with mysteries without knowing the attitude of faith toward

mystery is the modern manifestation of Gnosis. Gnosis is not to be understood as only a historical category, but as a universal one. It—and not atheism, which annihilates God because it must reject the hitherto existing images of God—is the real antagonist of the reality of faith.*

Equally modern is Buber's description in "The Foundation Stone" of "the lust for overrunning reality" which led the radical Sabbatians and the Frankists to revolt against the distinction between good and evil. The divided motivation which leads men to use evil for the sake of good may even lead to that Gnostic perversion which elevates evil into something holy in itself. The radical Sabbatians believed that they could redeem evil by performing it as if it were not evil, that is, by preserving an inner intention of purity in contrast to the deed. "That is an illusion," writes Buber, "for all that man does reacts on his soul, even when he fancies that his soul hovers over the deed." Man submits to illusion and becomes intoxicated with it, and as a result "he becomes at once completely agitated and crippled in his motive power." This demonic "lust for overrunning reality" is not simply a product of unbelief but a crisis within men's souls, a crisis of temptation, freedom, and dishonesty in which "the realms are overturned, everything encroaches on everything else, and possibility is more powerful than reality." The fascination with the demonic in modern literature, the tendency of many to turn psychoanalysis or "psychodrama"

* *Eclipse of God,* "Reply to C. G. Jung" (Harper's Torchbook), p. 136.

into a cult of self-realization, and the illusory belief that personal fulfillment can come through "release" of one's deep inward energies all show the peculiarly modern relevance of the "crisis of temptation and dishonesty" which Buber describes.

A second important key to understanding the essays in this volume, in addition to "holy insecurity," is Buber's attitude toward the redemption of evil. Redemption does not take place within the individual soul but in the world through the real meeting of God and man. Everything is waiting to be hallowed by man, for there is nothing so crass or base that it cannot become material for sanctification. "The profane," for Hasidism, is only a designation for the not yet hallowed. No renunciation of the object of desire is commanded: it is only necessary that man's relation to the object be hallowed in his life with nature, his work, his friendship, his marriage, and his solidarity with the community. Hence serving God with the "evil urge" and "hallowing the everyday" are essentially the same. "Hallowing transforms the urges by confronting them with holiness and making them *responsible* toward what is holy." Transforming the evil passion into good cannot take place inside oneself, but only in relation. It is just in his dialogue with others that man finds it possible to serve God with his fear, anger, love, and sexual desire. Serving God with the "evil urge" is like the "sublimation" of Freud's psychoanalysis in that it makes creative use of basic energies rather than suppressing them. But it differs from sublimation, as it is conceived by Freud, in that it takes place as a by-

16

product of the dialogue between man and man rather than as an essentially individual event in which the individual uses his relationship with others for his own self-realization. " 'Sublimation' takes place within the man himself," writes Buber, "the 'raising of the spark' takes place between man and the world."

The basis for the Hasidic attitude toward redemption is the belief that redemption, like creation, takes place at every moment. Man's work is enclosed in God's in such a way that each moment of redemption is perfect in itself as well as taking place in the time series of the world. These are not moments of "a mystical, timeless now." Each moment is filled with all time, for in it true presentness and the movement of history are united. This union of history and the moment involves a tension and a contradiction, for although redemption takes place at every moment, there is no definite moment in the present or the future in which the redemption of the world could be pronounced as having taken place once for all. "God's redeeming power is at work everywhere and at all times, but . . . a state of redemption exists nowhere and never." Redemption is not dependent upon Messianic calculations or any apocalyptic event, but on the unpremeditated turning of our whole world-life to God. This turning is open to the whole of mankind and to all ages, writes Buber, for all are face to face with redemption and all action for God's sake is Messianic action.

Judaism does not neglect spiritual inwardness, as Simone Weil believed, says Buber, but neither is it content with it. It demands that inward truth become real life if it is to remain truth: "A drop of Messianic consummation must be mingled with every hour; otherwise the hour is godless, despite all piety and devoutness." The corollary of this demand for the redemption of the world and not just of the individual soul is the refusal to accept the Gnostic rejection of creation—the division between the kingdom of this world and the kingdom of God which leaves the evil of the world forever unredeemable. "The world is reality, and it is reality created not to be overcome but to be hallowed." Redemption, to Buber and to Hasidism, always means redemption *of* evil and not *from* it, for evil is "the power which God created for his service and for the performance of his work." "This very world, this very contradiction, unabridged, unmitigated, unsmoothed, unsimplified, unreduced, this world shall be—not overcome—but consummated." We cannot call this world God's, says the Yehudi in Buber's Hasidic chronicle-novel *For the Sake of Heaven,* if it is to be forevermore divided between God and Satan. " 'Is it for this that He gave us a mouth which can convey the truth of our heart to an alien heart and a hand which can communicate to the hand of our recalcitrant brother something of the warmth of our very blood?' " Hasidism cannot accept a redemption in which half of the world will be eternally damned or cut off from God: "There can be no eternity in which *everything* will not be accepted into God's atonement." *

* I have made some use in these pages of material from my book *Martin Buber: The Life of Dialogue* (University of Chicago Press, 1955; Harper's Torchbooks, 1960), Chap. XVI—"The Eclipse of God"—and Chap. XVII—"The Redemption of Evil."

I wish to acknowledge my indebtedness to Rabbi Elisha Nattiv for providing me with the first draft of a translation of "Redemption" from Hebrew into English. Otherwise all the essays were translated from the German and are entirely my own translation. "Spinoza, Sabbatai Zvi, and the Baal-Shem" was first published as the foreword to the 1927 collection of Professor Buber's re-creations of Hasidic tales and teachings, *Die chassidischen Bücher*. "Spirit and Body of the Hasidic Movement" formed the main part of the introduction to Buber's *Der grosse Maggid und seine Nachfolge* ("The Great Maggid and His Followers"—1921). "Symbolic and Sacramental Existence" derives from a lecture that Professor Buber gave in 1934 at one of the Eranos sessions at Ascona, Switzerland; the rest of the essays proper were written in Jerusalem during the years 1940–1943, originally in Hebrew and then later in German. The Supplement, "Christ, Hasidism, Gnosis," was written in 1954 and first published in the Munich periodical *Merkur*.

MAURICE FRIEDMAN
*Bronxville, New York*
*1959*

# AUTHOR'S FOREWORD

This book has arisen in the course of many years as the slowly growing product of a long work of scholarship and interpretation in the great literature of the Hasidic teaching and legend.

More than fifty years ago I began to become acquainted with the writings of a great religious movement, Hasidism, of which as a boy through half-degenerate offshoots I had obtained a fleeting impression without realizing what it meant, or what it might one day mean for my own way of life.* Since then I have been striving toward an understanding of its truth, toward an understanding of that in it which has disclosed itself to me as truth. In this book, as in the first volume of *Hasidism and the Way of Man*, the essential results of this work are shown.

Together with two other of my books, *The Tales of*

* See Volume I, *Hasidism and Modern Man*, Book I—"Hasidism and Modern Man" and Book II—"My Way to Hasidism," pp. 21–69.—Ed.

*the Hasidim* \* and *For the Sake of Heaven. A Chronicle,*† the two volumes of *Hasidism and the Way of Man* form a unity of life and work. Of the three this is the one in which I directly and explicitly express the message to the human world that Hasidism did not want to be, but that it was and is. I consider the truth of Hasidism vitally important for Jews, Christians, and other men, and at this particular hour more important than ever before. For now is the hour when we are in danger of forgetting for what purpose we are on earth, and I know of no other teaching that reminds us of this so forcibly.

Hasidism has never set foot in the world of man as Christianity has done. Because of its truth and because of the great need of the hour, I carry it into the world against its will.

MARTIN BUBER
*Jerusalem*
*Spring 1959*

\* Vol. I, *The Early Masters* (New York: Schocken Books, 1947); Vol. II, *The Later Masters* (1948).
† Buber's Hasidic chronicle-novel published by Harper & Bros., 1953, and by Meridian Books (paperback), 1958.—Ed.

CHAPTER I

# THE BEGINNINGS

I         If one wishes to understand the appearance of Hasidism within Judaism's history of faith and its significance for the history of religion in general, one must not begin with its teachings as such. The Hasidic teaching, considered by itself, brings no new spiritual elements; it represents only a selection. Newly elaborated, to be sure, newly formulated, and newly composed into a new unity, it is still only a selection, on the one hand, from the late Kabbala, on the other hand, from popular traditions, and even the criterion that determined this selection is no theoretical one. What constitutes the uniqueness and the greatness of Hasidism is not a teaching, but a mode of life, a mode of life that shapes a community and that is consonant with community by its very nature. The relation between Hasidic teaching and the Hasidic mode of life, moreover, is by no means so constituted that the life is to be regarded as a realization of the teaching. On the contrary, it is rather the new mode of life that presses toward a conceptual expression, a theological explana-

24

tion, and just from this need stems the practical criterion that determines the selection of the elements. This also explains the fact that the originator of Hasidic theology, Dov Baer of Mezritch, does not call the founder of Hasidism, the Baal-Shem, his teacher, though the latter has taught him, as he relates, mysteries and "unifications," the language of birds and the writing of the angels. The Baal-Shem did not have new theological concepts to impart to him, but a living connection with this world and the world above.

The Baal-Shem belongs to those central figures of the history of religion whose effect on others has arisen through the fact that they *lived* in a certain way. These men did not proceed *from* a teaching, but moved *to* a teaching, in such a way that their life worked as a teaching, as a teaching not yet grasped in words. The life of such men requires a theological commentary to which their own words represent a contribution, but often only an entirely fragmentary one; at times they are to be used only as a kind of introduction—for these words, according to their intention, are by no means interpretations, but rather expressions of their life. Of the words of the Baal-Shem that are known to us, in so far as we may regard them as faithfully handed down to us, it is not the objective content that may be detached from them that is significant, but their character of pointing to a life.

Two things follow from this. First, that the whole personal attitude of faith that constitutes the essence of this life, works to form community. This does not mean forming a brotherhood, a separated order, removed from public life, which guards an esoteric teaching. It means, rather, forming community, forming a community of men who remain in families, station, and public activity. Some are more closely, some more loosely bound with the master, but all imprint in their own, free, public life the way of life that they have received through their intercourse with him. Included in this, naturally, is the decisive fact that the master does not live alone or in seclusion with a band of disciples, but in the world and with the world, and that just this, his life in the world and with the world, belongs to the innermost core of his relation of faith.

Within this community, secondly, arise a series of men with the same kind of life, men who have attained a related mode of life in part independently, but first receiving through the master the decisive impulse, the decisive moulding. These are men in different stages, of very different natures, but endowed with the self-same basic characteristic, that the teaching is carried onward by their life, to which all that they say is only a marginal notation. Each leads an individual life, that, for his part, forms community, therefore a life in the world and with the world, and one that, for its part, again gives birth, in spirit, to men of the same kind. These together form the core of the movement—the formation of community and the spiritual begetting of disciples who form communities and who therefore neither enter into seclusion nor break off the tradition. So long as both remain effective, the flowering of Hasidism continues, that is, some five generations beyond the Baal-Shem. The communities were by no means communities of model men, and even their leaders were definitely not what one calls a saint in Christianity or Buddhism. But the communities were communities, and the leaders were leaders. The "zaddikim" of these five generations form together a group of religious personalities of a vitality, a spiritual powerfulness, and a manifold originality such as, to my knowledge, have nowhere in the history of religions been concentrated in so short a span of time. But the most important fact about them is that each of them was surrounded by a community that lived a brotherly life and was able to live it through the fact that a leader was there who brought them all closer together by bringing them closer to that in which they believed. In an otherwise not very productive century—even in Eastern Europe—the "unenlightened" Polish and Ukrainian Jewry brought forth the greatest phenomenon in the history of the spirit, greater than any individual genius in art and in thought: a society that lives by its faith.

Because this is so, because Hasidism in the first instance is not a category of teaching, but one of life, our chief source of knowledge of Hasidism is its legends, and only after them comes its theoretical literature. The latter is the commentary, the former the text, even though a text that has been handed down in a state of extreme corruption, one that is incapable of being restored in its purity. It is foolish to protest that the legend does not convey to us the reality of Hasidic life. Naturally, the legend is no chronicle, but it is truer than the chronicle for those who know how to read it. One cannot reconstruct from it, certainly, the factual course of events. But despite its corruption, one can perceive in it the life-element in which the events were consummated, the element that received them and with naïve enthusiasm told them and told them again until they became legend.

Apart from secondary literary elaborations, which betray themselves as such at the first glance, no arbitrariness rules in this telling. What impels the narrator is an inner compulsion whose nature is of the Hasidic life, the blood-warm Hasidic connection of leader and community. Even the boldest miracle stories are not, for the most part, the product of cold invention: the zaddik has done the unheard-of with unheard-of power that transformed the souls of those present, and they experienced its working as a miracle; they could not report it otherwise than in the language of miracle. It is usually pointed out, further, that some of these stories are of far older origin; much of what is told of early Talmudic masters we find here again as deeds of the zaddikim. But even this crude absence of historical foundation has its share in the truth. That in past tradition which was related to present blessing was interwoven with this present by the naïve mind that experienced it—the thought of falsification lay far from their minds; the old stories were universally known, in fact. Rather there arose of itself the report that the rabbi has now performed that well-known deed anew, not in order to imitate the first doer, but in complete spontaneity, because there are, in fact, certain basic forms of good works. How, for example, could the irrepressible desire to assist helpless creatures be expressed

28

more directly than if the rabbi comes late to communal prayer because he had to comfort a weeping child? Or the inner freedom from possessions more radically than if, before he goes to sleep, the rabbi declares all that he has for anyone who wishes it, so that the thief who might come in the night should remain free of the burden of sin? But for the most part one finds that in the retelling something new and characteristic has come into these stories. What was handed down was by its very nature an event from individual life; transported into the atmosphere of communal living, it becomes something different.

**II**     One can only understand the origin of the new principle of life that appears in the Hasidic movement if one calls to mind how the Sabbatian catastrophe worked itself out among the Jews of Poland and the Ukraine. From there arose, a quarter of a century after the death of Sabbatai Zvi, the strongest eruption of the hope which had continued to well up despite the great disillusionment. The form that this eruption took was the wanderings to Palestine of the band of penitents led by Yehuda Hasid, wanderings almost reminiscent of certain by-products of the crusades. Here the Sabbatian disintegration of the teaching, which Gershom Scholem has rightly called a religious nihilism, attained its most extreme consequence in the form of the Frankist sect, probably the most remarkable configuration of the spiritual lie in modern history. And here too arose its counter-movement, Hasidism. By "counter-movement" I do not mean an external battle against the external manifestation, but the potential of opposing strength, ascending out of the depths of organic communal life, the education of new community cells of new kinds in opposition to those that were decaying and threatening the organism with decay, the rebirth of a healthy capacity for faith in a people mortally ill through the perversion of their faith.

From this it already follows that this movement could not by its nature be a reformation. It could not wish to lead back to an earlier, unproblematic state, to the state before the illness. It begins with the conflict of elements now existing and creates the inner antidote out of just this material, the very material from which the inner poison was brewed. It is not without significance, in this connection, that the decisive development of Hasidism did not occur after that of Frankism, but at the same time.

We owe to the work of Gershom Scholem * the knowledge and understanding of Sabbatian theology that enables us to grasp the dialectic of movement and counter-movement in post-Sabbatian spiritual history. We knew that uncanny historical fact, Sabbatai Zvi, the appearance of the Messianic pretender, who, after all the No's that generations of people awaiting the Messiah had given his predecessors, received the jubilant Yes of the masses and who now, crowned and wor-

* Gershom Scholem, *Major Trends in Jewish Mysticism* (New York: Schocken Books, 2nd Ed., 1951), Chap. VIII.

shipped as the holy King, abandoned Judaism. Now we know too the still more uncanny theology that, familiar with all the artifices of a gnostic perversion of values, reinterpreted the meaning of the event into its opposite: the Messiah must enter completely into the interior of the *kelipa,* the demonic power of the shells, in order to liberate the holiness held captive there. In doing this he fulfills the purpose of the exile of Israel and redeems Israel and the world in one. And even that is not enough: the "holy" sin becomes a standard; one must hurl oneself into sin in order to tear from it the holy sparks. Already there is no longer any sin. With the fulfillment of the meaning of the new, the Messianic aeon, the yoke of the old Torah, valid only for the unredeemed world, is broken. The new revelation that permits all, that sanctifies all is here.

The alienation of Messianism, its saturation with gnosis, was prepared in the Kabbalistic eschatology, but it has unmistakably reached its high point here. In prophetic faith the Messiah was the perfected man who stepped forth out of Israel and, as the representative of God, did the work reserved for man; in the fragment of a Jewish-Christian gospel, we still find the conception of a God who "awaits" the Coming One "in all the Prophets." In apocalyptic literature and later in the Kabbala, this dramatic over-against-ness of God and man, on which the faith of Israel is grounded, is more and more dissolved. Divine emanations mediate between heaven and earth, and it is one of them which descends as Messiah to the world of man. Finally Sabbatai is prayed to as "the true God and king of the world." It is only logical when he, like the Gnostic Christ, enters into the hell of this world and makes himself like its rulers in order to conquer them. But the conception, taken over from the later Kabbala, of drawing forth the holy sparks out of the impurity is, in the final analysis, still of a Jewish, not a syncretistic origin. That man's relation with God, who indeed "dwells in the midst of their impurities," purifies and hallows all, that man must serve God with the evil urge, that redemption overcomes the distinction between pure and impure, sacred and profane, and *all* becomes pure and holy—these we may regard as an autochthonous possession of Jewish faith. The ingredients for the antidote are ready.

Sabbatian theology anticipated the redeemed world: it capitalized for present use on the instructions for what should become reality in a still inconceivable future perfection of the world. In doing this it undermined the Torah and deprived it of its living substance. For Torah is only present in a substantial and living manner where man is shown a way as the way of God, and showing a way always signifies, in any existence that we can imagine, exclusion of all that which is not this way. That *all* becomes the way in the world of perfection can only be properly grasped in the Messianic expectation and preparation. If one treats it as a completed fact while surrounded by the facts of the unredeemed world—facts more powerful than all theology, then one literally stands on the zero point, on *nihil* and is, if one remains honest, already finished. But from this point on a twofold possibility emerges.

The one is that of the perfect lie: amid the changing of nothing, it can move with juggling gestures, as if it were something. The other is that which is open to him who begins something, namely a new mode of life. Both, Jacob Frank and the Baal-Shem, proceed from the post-Sabbatian situation behind which one can no longer go. The one dashes the undermined Torah to pieces, the other fills it with life.

# III

When I say, "the perfect lie," I by no means wish to suggest by that that one can comprehend Frank if one understands him to be an impostor: that would be a misleading oversimplification. By "lie" I do not mean here something that the man says or does, but what he is; this man is not a liar, rather he is a lie. That does not mean, therefore, that he does not believe in himself; but he believes in himself in the manner of the lie, as the lie believes in itself—for even the lie has a way of believing in itself. Sabbatai clearly believes in something absolute, and he believes in himself in relation to it; in it rests his "Messianic consciousness." It is not his belief in general, but his belief in himself that does not stand firm. That later a compromise between the two is established alters nothing in the fact that at the decisive moment the link has snapped: Sabbatai has not decided to pay for the possibility of miracle with the possibility of martyrdom.

Frank, who did not grow up like Sabbatai in an atmosphere of ascetic longing for redemption, but in one of a Marrano libertinism, Frank, who does not end his public activity with apostasy, but begins with it, can certainly not fall like Sabbatai since he does not stand like him. He does not believe in something absolute and in himself in relation to it; rather he believes in nothing. He cannot believe genuinely even in himself, but only in the manner of the lie, through filling the space of nothing with himself. For the sake of appearance, indeed, he populates the nothing with divine shapes, the spawn of late-Gnostic fantasy, like "The Three" who lead the world and the hidden "Big Brother" unknown even to him. But it is evident that he only plays with this mythological world. Actually he holds to nothing except himself, and he manages to hold to himself without having any sort of foothold in reality. Therefore, he no longer has any restraint, and his absence of restraint is his magic with which he works on the men on whom he wants to work.

Frank's very nature precludes the question whether he was mentally ill or healthy. He has a real delusion, the delusion that produces absence of restraint, but he utilizes this real delusion in order to work magically on men—and he needs the magically compelling effect on them not merely for his current aims; he needs it ever more because the nihilistic belief in himself, threatened by the crisis of self-awareness, must nourish itself from the belief of others to be able to continue to exist. When, to win back the power that was slipping away from him, Frank sends word from the town of Offenbach to his adherents in Poland that Jacob the true and living God lives and will live for ever, this craving to be believed in so that he may be able to believe has reached its highest intensity. As the Messianism of Israel was abolished in Sabbatianism, so the Sabbatian Messianism of emanations is abolished here: neither God nor His emanations any longer exists; there now exists only the human person who fills the nothing. At the same time, the man who conceives of himself as this person must incessantly take into himself the warm flesh and blood of other people's belief in him to be able to persist himself. But the demonic community of the demonic messiah—the group of disciples that surround him and that allow themselves to be consumed by him with their orgies and rapture—announces from within the shelter of the Christian church the decay of the community of Israel. The strong life of the Jewish community had been inundated by the Sabbatian torrent; out of this torrent there emerges its caricature, the counter-community. This band, at once unfettered yet wholly bound to a leader who leads them into nothing, affords an unsurpassable spectacle of disintegration.

IV    Hasidism, just like Frankism, starts from the situation created by the Sabbatian catastrophe, but not in order to carry it further. There is no going further in this direction except into corruption and destruction. What has happened is recognized as a catastrophe, and, indeed, not as one within the people or within the world alone, but as one of the bond between God and Israel, between God and man. The bond between God and mankind has experienced a serious injury, the seemingly most intimate nearness has revealed itself as abuse; what appeared to be full authority issued into betrayal. The calamity in the relationship between above and below still swells, the lie becomes mighty and poses as the new truth. It not only threatens to ensnare in delusion and guilt the deeply confused Jewry that has now become rootless, not merely to undermine its inward and outward structure, but also to burst open a chasm between it and God, deeper than any that has ever existed. Here begins the new element that is represented in the mode of life of the Baal-Shem and his followers. It is not only a question of the healing of the people, but of healing the broken relationship between heaven and earth. The evil must be checked before it becomes invincible. But this cannot take place through battle, but only through new mediation and new leading.

It is no accident that the Hasidic movement arose in Podolia. From the days of Sabbatai Zvi until the time of the birth of the Baal-Shem, Podolia had belonged to Turkey, and the Jews of Turkey had been especially exposed to the problems that arose in the wake of Sabbatianism. Here too, later, Frank first gained a foothold. The Baal-Shem must be understood from the standpoint of this people, shaken by the shivering fever-fit of the abysmal hour. The seclusion of his youth in the stillness of the Carpathians appears like a sym-

bol of his gathering the strength to resist the temptation. When he steps forth, it is in order to effect the
healing of the body and of the soul. Characteristic of
this is the legend of how he won over the great Maggid
of Mezritch, the man who was to develop further his
teaching. First he helps him conquer a bodily illness.
But then he shows him that his knowledge is no knowledge, and there now follows a manifestation that the
recipient experiences with a complete shattering of the
soul as an event similar to a vision.

Such winning of men for the new mode of life, the
formation of a circle dispersed over the country and
nonetheless centered in him, a circle of men at once
rejoicing in the world and striving for nearness to God,
is the Baal-Shem's real work. In the last period of his
life and afterward, this work stood in opposition to the
activities of the Frankists. That he should have taken
part in the disputation of the rabbis against the latter
sect is not merely unhistorical, but also inwardly un-
true. His true attitude appears in the following legend:
Once on the eve of the Day of Atonement the Baal-
Shem was so overcome by the thought of the danger
that threatened Israel of losing along with the oral
Torah its whole life in the tradition that he had to stop
in the midst of blessing the community. He threw himself down before the Ark and indicted the rabbis who
had not guarded in the right manner the good entrusted to them. The next day during the closing
prayer, he was transported to the gate of heaven. There
he found the prayers of half a century that had not
gained admission. He sought out the Messiah, and

with his help succeeded in entering with the prayers. Thus amidst great joy in heaven the doom was overcome.

The important motif in this legend is that the prayers of fifty years had to remain lying on earth until they were raised to the gate of heaven on this Day of Atonement through the powerful praying of the community of the Baal-Shem. Thus the prayers of the rabbinic community in the Sabbatian epoch did not rise of themselves and needed uplifting by the new movement. In fact, the Baal-Shem stands with his life and thought not only against Frankism, but also against the rabbinate of the time, whom he accused of having removed the people from nearness to God through estranging the Torah from life and of having by this made the people susceptible to the false message of God's nearness. The Baal-Shem died soon after the mass baptisms of the Frankists; it is told how he lamented shortly before his death over the "severed limbs of the Shekina," of the glory of God dwelling in the world. The legend tells that he had to die just because of that heaven-storming venture.

We shall come to understand the relation of the Baal-Shem to Sabbatianism still more deeply, however, if we take note of the intimations of the legend concerning a temptation that approached him from that source. In a remarkably reserved manner that clearly passes over important facts in silence, the legend reports that once Sabbatai Zvi appeared to the Baal-Shem and beseeched him to redeem him. In order to effect a redemption of this sort, one must unite all the elements of one's own

38

being with those of the dead man, as Elisha lay on the dead boy with all his limbs; one must bind each of the three elements of one's own soul—the breath of life, the spirit, and the soul—with the corresponding element of the one in need of redemption. The Baal-Shem wanted to fulfill the request; but since he feared the influence of so intimate a contact with evil, he began the work cautiously, not all at once but distributed over a period. During this time Sabbatai, evidently counting on the intimacy that had arisen between the two of them, came to him once in sleep and wanted to tempt him— the narrator does not say how, but it is not difficult to fill in what is not said: the false messiah wants to tempt him to hold and declare himself to be the Messiah. But the Baal-Shem withstood him and slung him from him with such great force that he plunged to the bottom of the underworld. The Baal-Shem later said of him that there had been a holy spark in him, but that Satan had caught him in his snare, the snare of pride. In conjunction with this tale, one must keep in mind the fact that the Baal-Shem used to warn that in stretching out one's feet before drawing one's last breath, one should feel no self-satisfaction. According to tradition, he was heard to whisper before his death the verse from the Psalms, "Let not the foot of pride come near me!"

The well-known philosopher of history Spengler, referring to my work, wished to see in the Baal-Shem the type of a Messiah. That accords neither with the consciousness of the man nor with his existence. Nothing in him is eschatological, nothing in him presses the claim to be something final, conclusive. Nowhere do we hear from his mouth words of the sort that we meet ever again in the "messiahs," from those of the purest stamp to the most impure, from Jesus to Jacob Frank: "I have come in order to . . ." In events of various kinds the legends depict the Baal-Shem as learning that his hour is not the hour of redemption, but of a renewal. In these stories he also never appears as the One, the perfected man; he only seeks to help the redemption, to prepare for it, and this too in vain. One legend hints that in the future when the Messiah comes, it will be he, namely the reincarnated Israel ben Eliezer. But in this present life his nature is another and his task another. Everything in him stands opposed to the "hastening of the End," which has degenerated into delusion and lies and has brought the relationship to God into the extremest peril through frantic devotion to sham gods. Everything points to the necessity of now attaining once again to a beginning, the beginning of a real life for the real God in the real world.

V       It is customary to regard so-called zaddikism as a later degeneration of Hasidism; but what is described thus is only the excess development of an element which is to be found in all clarity in the early period of the movement, an element without which its foundations are unthinkable.

Hasidism found the concept of the zaddik already

in existence in Kabbalistic literature as well as in the popular tradition, but it brought to it a new content. In the Kabbala he signified a man united in a special manner with God, therefore not only beholding His mystery, but also acting as His representative. In Hasidism he has, in addition, become the man who leads the community in God's place, the man who mediates between God and the community. By community is to be understood always both the definite, limited community of this individual zaddik and the community of all Israel. The latter is represented in the former: the individual community is the entire people.

This development of a special type into an institution is to be understood from the standpoint of the crisis. The more acute the crisis became the more emphatically was posed the question concerning the new leadership. The old rabbinic leadership, despite isolated energetic thrusts, had not been able to master the crisis because it only fought for the preservation of the teaching and not for the renewal of life. Already in the beginnings of Hasidism it was regarded in Hasidic circles much as the people regard a government that has prepared no defense against an enemy invasion and can now offer it no resistance; one must set up a counter-government. This means the zaddik in his new Hasidic imprint. He can no longer, of course, be primarily a scholar. The founders of the movement were very much intent, to be sure, on bringing important Talmudists into their camp. But this was accomplished in each case—as the legend relates of Baer of Mezritch in the house of the Baal-Shem—through

41

criticism of his former mode of life and introduction into another. It involved, therefore, an inner transformation which removed to the periphery what had formerly been the center of his existence while the new service took possession of the center. This service is one of the strongest fusions of intercourse with God and intercourse with man that is known to the history of religions: one serves God through helping His creatures, one helps the creatures through leading them to God, and this leading does not go beyond life but right through it. Discipleship in the house of the founder of the movement was education for leadership.

Stirred in his innermost core by the Sabbatian revolution, shaken to his foundations by its outcome, the Polish Jew longed passionately for leadership, for a man who would take him under his wing, give certainty to his bewildered soul, give order and shape to his chaotic existence, who would make it possible for him again both to believe and to live. The Hasidic movement educated such leaders. Rabbis who only bestowed advice as to how the prescriptions of the law should be applied could no longer satisfy the new longing, but sermons on the meaning of the teaching also did not help. In a world in which one could no longer muster the strength for reflection and decision, a man was needed to show one how to believe and to say what was to be done. When we consider the unconditional devotion of the Frankists to Frank, we see how utterly men lost themselves to one who was ready to take from them entirely their responsibility. The Hasidic movement had to begin here. It had to put forward men who would take on their strong shoulders each one who wanted to be borne, but would set them on the ground again as soon as they could be expected to get on by themselves. In utter opposition to the pseudo-Messianic types, these men themselves took responsibility for the souls entrusted to them and yet did not allow the sparks of responsibility to be extinguished in them. Frank, like Sabbatai, wanted to be understood as a fulfillment and dissolution of the Torah. But the highest praise that could be bestowed on a zaddik was that he was a Torah, that is, that in his make-up, in his every-day gestures, in his unemphatic, unarbitrary, unintentional actions and attitudes, "in the way he tied and untied his sandals," was represented that in the Torah which is inexpressible but which can be transmitted through human existence. These men mediated between God and man, but they pointed men with great seriousness to that immediate relationship to God that no mediation can replace.

A further important distinguishing mark is the multiplicity of zaddikim. The Messianic pretender is, by his nature, a single figure; the institution of the zaddik is represented, by its nature, in a multiplicity of contemporary living men among whom, as it were, the community is divided. As there are thirty-six hidden zaddikim, says a statement ascribed to the Baal-Shem, so there are thirty-six manifest ones. Despite all excesses, no zaddik holds himself to be the only one, despite all quarrels between community and community, all jealousy between teacher and disciples, this division remains irrevocably valid. Certainly, Hasidim believe and say at times that outside their rabbi there is none in the world; but the basic view of the first zaddikim is visible when a zaddik describes this behavior as idol worship. "How then should one speak?" he asks and answers, "One should say: 'Our rabbi is the best for our needs!'" That means, each particular zaddik and his Hasidim are destined for each other.

"I have come to help the whole world," says Frank. The zaddik has to help his Hasidim. But in order really to help them, in order to bring them to God with their whole lives—not merely something of them, their thought, their feelings, but their whole lives—he must embrace their whole lives, from their concern about bread to their concern about the purification of the soul. He does not have to do *some*thing for them, but *every*thing. And because he shall do all, he must be capable of all. "Why," it is jestingly asked, "is the zaddik called 'the good Jew'? If one wished to say that he prays well, then one would have to call him a 'good prayer'; if one wished to say that he learns well, a 'good learner.' A 'good Jew' thinks well and drinks well and eats well and works well and means well and does everything well."

The legend of the Baal-Shem symbolizes the vital connection of the zaddik with the community by showing him dancing with his Hasidim or telling how his teaching-discourse in their assembly appeared to each individual as directed to him and as counsel for his personal life. But already in the first Hasidic book we find, based on sayings of the Baal-Shem, a complete formulation of this connection. In it the reciprocity of

44

the tie is given the strongest possible emphasis. Certainly the community in itself is what the earth was before it was joined with heaven: a chaos; but "the zaddikim may not say that they do not need the mass of the people." The mass of the people is like the bearers of the Ark of the Covenant without whom it cannot move even though in truth it is it that bears its bearers. On the other hand, sharp criticism was made of the condition existing before Hasidism and continuing alongside the movement, in which the learned man, on the one side, and the mass of the people, on the other, represent two "ends" far removed from each other which enter into no relationship with each other: the learned must become aware of their own lacks, which indicate to them that they should take part in the life of the mass of people. Only then can they also uplift them.

# VI

But this by no means implies that only a receptive function is accorded the "simple man." Rather, according to the Hasidic view, an element of highest active significance is to be found just in him.

Here too we can best proceed from Frankism. Jacob Frank states time after time to his followers that he is an *am-haaretz,* an ignorant man. "God has chosen me," he says, "because I am an *am-haaretz.*" What is in question here is not accorded to the sage and the learned, but "only to such ignorant men as I, for the sage look up to heaven, although they see nothing there, but we shall look at the earth." In a beautiful parable, which of all his sayings comes closest to the Hasidic parables, he tells of the perfect pearl that none of the masters could pierce because none dared to do so. Each master knew how easily the pearl could be ruined in so doing, but a journeyman who did not know the danger undertook the task in the absence of his master and succeeded.

But just here, in the seemingly greatest proximity, the decisive difference between the world of Frank and that of the Baal-Shem can be recognized.

Frank praises his ignorance because it frees him from restraint. He is bound by no knowledge of the Torah. He does not know the divine difficulty of human responsibility, therefore his hand does not tremble when it pierces the pearl of the human world. He is simply chosen; he does not need to seek the truth as to what to do and what to leave undone, he does not need to decide, all is decided. "I have been chosen," he says, "because I am an *am-haaretz*, and as such I shall, with God's help, pierce all and bring to all." Later he no longer even says, "with God's help." He himself is "that burning thornbush."

The simple man whom the Hasidic legend praises has no dram of self-satisfaction. He would imagine himself mocked if anyone said to him that he was chosen. He too does not need to decide, but just because he lives his life simply and directly without brooding, accepts the world as it is. Wherever the opportunity offers itself to him, he accomplishes with unperturbed soul the good that is entrusted to him in such a manner as if he had known it from all eternity. But if he should go astray some time, he seeks the way out with strong strides and casts his lot on God. It is God he is concerned about. He is his great Lord and his great friend; he constantly addresses Him as Lord and friend, he tells Him all as if he did not yet know about it; he is not shy before Him. He can neither learn nor "properly" pray, that is, with *kavanot*, with secret intentions. But he does his daily work eagerly and while doing it recites the psalms that he knows by heart; this too is address, and he is sure that it is heard. But at times when his heart is especially full, he whistles in honor of God or dances and leaps because he cannot show his love for Him in any other way. And God rejoices in it. He rejoices in him. This Hasidic God knows how to rejoice, like his Hasidim. But more than this: it happens at times, according to the legends, that such a man who "does not know how to pray," pours out his soul before God with all his might in the midst of the praying of the congregation and with the strength of his praying bears upward all weak and lame-winged prayers. He too has the unifying strength.

It is told of a great sufferer, prayer, and music-lover among the Hasidim, Rabbi Israel of Kosnitz, that he was especially pleased when the "simple people" came to him; when his disciples asked him the reason for this, he said to them, "I—all my effort and work is directed toward becoming simple, and they are simple already."

And because the "simple man" is so important, so long as the movement continues in its original strength and purity there can be—in contrast to the Kabbala—no Hasidic esoteric. There is no sealing away of the mysteries; everything is fundamentally open to all, and everything is reiterated again and again so simply and concretely, that each man of real faith can grasp it. It has been rightly pointed out how much the Hasidic recognition of the formerly despised *am-haaretz* as a member of the community with equal religious rights and the Hasidic admiration of the man of simple faith have furthered the growth of the movement. But one must add to this that already in its beginnings the movement is borne in the broader circles of the people by a new generation, indeed by a new type of man, who will no longer have anything to do with the fateful "hastening of the end" and undertakes to serve God in the given life hour with such strength as he possesses. The movement strove, further, to elevate this type of man in the eyes of the people and thus to supplement the new spiritual authority of the zaddikim by the religious elite itself arising out of the mass of the people.

# VII

Frank based his glorification of his own ignorance on the assertion that the former way, that of knowledge of the law and of the teachings of faith, will now be replaced by a new way "that never yet, since the beginning of the world, occurred to a man." The old words are "long dead," the laws must "be dashed to pieces like a potsherd," everything from the past must fall before the new building, that shall endure forever, can be erected. "The Christ known to you has said that he has come in order to liberate the world from the hands of Satan, but I have come in order to liberate it from all precepts and ordinances that have existed till now. I must annihilate all that; then will the good God reveal Himself" (that is, entirely in accordance with the customary Gnostic conception, the hidden God who is not identical with the creator and ruler of the world). Therefore Frank demanded of his followers that they should "wash themselves clean of all laws as the high priest washed himself clean before he entered the Holy of Holies"; they must strip off all that bound them to laws and teachings of faith and follow after him step by step. But once he made a statement that recalls what is told of the views of those who held the highest rank within the sect of the Assassins and that, according to recently published communications, can also be regarded as the true creed of the Nazis, the world-historical Assassins of our day: "All leaders must be without religion."

Here too Hasidism takes the situation of the crisis as its starting-point and does not go behind it. The Torah as law in the customary sense, that is, as the sum of the commands of God that have no other aim than enabling man to fulfill God's incomprehensible will, is placed in question by the Sabbatian antinomianism. The Hasidic movement cannot begin with the goal of restoring them in this sense. It can and will preserve the Torah only by converting the fixed boundary between

49

the spheres of bidden and forbidden things, on the one hand, and the indifferent things of the "adiaphora," on the other, into a flowing one. The Hasidic conception of the Torah is an elaboration of the traditional belief that God wants to win through man the world created by Him. He wants to make it truly His world, His kingdom, but through human deed. The intention of the divine revelation is to form the men who work on the redemption of creation. By this is not meant an isolated Messianic action, but a deed of the everyday that prepares the Messianic completion: the eschato-logical fever of the crisis here seems to be replaced by an equal value of all functions, which means, however, not simply health, but healing. The *mitzvot,* the com-mands, designate the realm of things that are already explicitly given to man for hallowing. Hasidism de-velops the late-Kabbalistic theory of the divine sparks that have fallen into the things and can be "uplifted" by man. It is for such uplifting that the *mitzvot* are en-joined to man. He who performs a *mitzva* with perfect *kavana,* that is, he who accomplishes the action in such a manner that his whole existence is concentrated in it and is directed in it to God, works on the hallowing of the world, on its conquest for God. But the sparks that need lifting rest not only in the things to which the *mitzvot* point. The demarcation between the sacred, that is, that which is designated for hallowing, and the profane, that which still lacks such specific designation, is a provisional one. The Torah indicates the circum-ference of revelation as it is till now. It lies with man whether and how much it will further expand. "Why,"

50

asks a zaddik, "do we speak of 'the time when the Torah *is* given' and not of 'the time when the Torah *was* given'? God wills that everything be hallowed until in the Messianic age the distinction between sacred and profane no longer exists because all has become holy." Here again Hasidism has apparently attained the closest proximity to Sabbatian Theology, as could not but be the case since it proceeds with the greatest seriousness from the situation defined by it, and here again its unconditional opposition to it is to be discerned. In the Messianic hour the partition between bidden and forbidden will not be removed and the Torah thereby abolished, but the Messianic hour will mark the *completion* of the work of permeating all things and all life with holiness, and the now-completed Torah will embrace the whole life. Indeed, nothing will exist any longer except that existence into which the Torah has entered and in which it has become living.

A saying from the early period of Hasidism comments on the text, "Be holy for I the Lord your God am holy": Now the holiness of Israel comes from the *mitzvot,* as one prays, "You have hallowed us through Your commandments," but in the time for which, according to the Talmudic teaching it is promised that the *mitzvot* will be suspended, the holiness of Israel will come directly from God. And a late saying draws the consequences of this by explaining why in the verse of the Bible which warns the people against "making woodcarving, shapes of all that the Lord thy God bid you," it says "bid" and not "forbid": one shall not make an idol out of any *mitzva;* seen from the kingdom of God, each is in suspense. On the other hand, there is no thing and no event of which I could say that it is not that which should be hallowed by me; on this rung of believing reality nothing indifferent can any longer be found. As the traditional hierarchy of persons is overcome by the acceptance of the *am-haaretz,* so the traditional hierarchy of actions is overcome by the religious acceptance of the "adiaphora." Even the *kavanot* elaborated by the late Kabbala for prayers for the unification of God and His Shekina, recede into the background for him who, as one of the most important thinkers of Hasidism said of himself, "prays with the floor and the bench." The great *kavana* is not joined to any particular selection of the prescribed: everything that is done with *kavana* can be the right, the redeeming act. Each action can be the one on which all depends; what is decisive is only the strength and concentration of hallowing with which I do it. To the question of what had been the most essential matter for his late teacher, a disciple answered, "Always just what he was engaged in at the moment."

# VIII

Jacob Frank used to say of his star, the star that, as he loved to quote from the prophecy of Balaam, "came forward out of Jacob," that all despised and common things were in the power of this star, and that only by going wholly into it could one attain salvation. One must first descend to the very bottom of the

Jacob's ladder, which consists of two sloping ladders that meet on earth, before one can ascend it. It is a question of making the alien fire, the fire of "sin," so much one's own that one can offer it to God; the alien fire, the fire with which Aaron's sons sacrificed, is nothing in comparison with what is to be done there. Therefore one must enter altogether into Edom, where the "strange actions" (a designation that is often found among the Sabbatians) do not prevail secretly, as in Israel, but openly. Jacob may not content himself, as before, with following Esau's footsteps; he must become one flesh with him. Esau or Edom is to be understood here at once literally, as Frank proclaimed through the mass baptism of his followers and through his Apology, and symbolically: it stands for the Kingdom of Sin into the very depths of which one must penetrate in order to overpower it. One must, as the Sabbatian statement goes, conquer the *kelipa* in their own house, one must fill the impurity with the strength of holiness until it bursts open from within. The great fortress, thus Frank expresses it in a characteristic image, cannot be conquered by all the arts of siege until an *am-haaretz* sneaks in at night through the sewer and seizes it.

The Frankist doctrine of the "strange actions" stands over against the Hasidic doctrine of the "alien thoughts." Here too the Hasidim proceed from the same common presuppositions: the abyss has opened, it is not for any man to live any longer as though evil did not exist. One cannot serve God merely by avoiding evil; one must engage oneself with it. The decisive difference here consists in the insight that in this engagement the shattering of the shells stands not at the end, but ever again, time after time, at the beginning. The sparks of God's light, in their deepest exile that we call evil, yearn for liberation. Burdened with their shells, from which they cannot separate themselves, they come to us as "alien thoughts," as desires. They come at all hours, even in those of prayer, indeed, especially in them, for they act in common with the *kelipot* and cannot do otherwise: the *kelipot* never have so great a greed to cause us to fall than when we cleave to God in prayer, and the sparks of holiness never yearn so much as then for our deed since then our redeeming strength is greatest. But the realization of their longing cannot take place otherwise than in the form of the *kelipa*, in the form of temptation, in other words, in the fantasy. The old saying, the greater a person is so much the greater is his urge, is modified: from the greatness of the temptation a soul recognizes how holy it is in its roots. Imagination is the power in us that is bound with the appearance of the sparks; and because these appearances arise out of the mixture of good and evil, one can say of imagination that it is the tree of the knowledge of good and evil.

Here decision takes place in each man, and on it redemption depends. Therefore, we should not push the alien thought away from us as something burdensome and offensive and thus cast off the holy sparks. Their appearance signifies an appearance of God in the things that are seemingly farthest from Him, as it is written (Jeremiah 31, 2): "The Lord has appeared to me from afar." We should receive this appearance willingly and do what it demands of us: in the sphere of our fantasy to liberate the pure passion from its object which limits it and direct it to the limitless; thereby we shatter the shell and redeem the spark that was imprisoned in it. Certainly the man who has to do with evil in this manner runs a great risk, and many zaddikim have warned that it is reserved to the holy man to pass through this danger. But to this it is objected that each man is in the world in order to work on the purification and redemption of the world. But to be able to hold one's ground against the danger, he must judge himself daily: in the fire of such judgment the innermost heart shall become ever stronger and the might of the *kelipa* cannot harm it.

Here, in the realm of the "alien thoughts," the object toward which desire is directed in the fantasy of man must become transparent, as it were, so that it may lose its demonic nature and set the glance free to turn to God. It is otherwise in the realm of the natural existence of man—his life with nature, his work, his friendship, his marriage, his understanding with the community: there the objects of inclination and of joy, which are just reality, not possibility, shall remain for one in their full reality. One may and should live genuinely with all, but one should live with it in consecration, one should hallow all that one does in his natural life. No renunciation is commanded. One eats in consecration, one savors one's taste of food in consecration, and the table becomes an altar. One works in consecration and lifts the sparks that are hidden in all tools.

55

One walks over the fields in consecration, and the silent songs of all creatures, those they speak to God, enter into the song of one's own soul. One drinks to one's companions in consecration, each to the other, and it is as if one studied together with them in the Torah. One dances in consecration, and a splendor radiates over the community. A man is united with his wife in consecration, and the Shekina rests over them.

The love between man and woman is a high principle of existence in the Kabbala, as is well known, not merely because the Kabbala represents by this image the uniting of the *sefirot,* the spheres that have emanated, and also the decisive union between God and the Shekina, but also because it is held to be of basic importance for the sake of redemption that the holy souls that have not yet completed their earthly wandering be embodied through conception and birth and drawn into the terrestrial world. Probably nothing else can make the antitheticalness of the manifestations after the Sabbatian crisis clearer to us than when we juxtapose what became of that conception in Frankism and what in Hasidism. I can here give only one characteristic example of each.

In the chronicle of Frank's deeds set down by his disciples, it is told how Frank during his imprisonment in Czenstochowa, where he enjoyed a very far-reaching freedom, directed to the women of his circle, who were called the "Sisters," the request that they select one from among them as the representative of all and deliver her to him. He would take her to himself and she would be blessed by the birth of a daughter. His wife who was present offered herself for this, but he rejected her because she was destined to bear sons and not daughters. The "Sisters" could not reach a unanimous conclusion since the rivalries among them were too great to be overcome, and after a violent wrangle, they asked the "holy Lord" that he himself should make the choice. Frank fell into a great wrath that lasted some weeks.

Over against this grotesque event, whose specific religious background is, however, unmistakable, I set a minor occurrence that I have taken from the notes of a grandson of Rabbi Mordecai of Stashov about the life of his grandfather. Rabbi Mordecai was at first a disciple of Rabbi Elimelech of Lisensk and after his death a disciple of the "Seer" of Lublin. This latter said to him once, "We shall now hand over to you a few hundred Jews so that you yourself can have a community to lead." Rabbi Mordecai replied that he wished to consult with his wife. When he came home and told his wife of the offer, she cried, "Gently, gently, let us first be Jews ourselves!" He now returned to the Lubliner, explained to him that he could not accept his offer, and adduced as cause the statement of his wife. When the Seer had heard this, he said, "From now on do not come any longer to me on the holidays, but stay with your wife. The holy souls wait for you two."

CHAPTER **II**

# THE FOUNDATION STONE

I Hasidism, like early Christianity, has at times been described as a result of the *am-haaretz*, that is, the uneducated "country people," the strata of the people who do not occupy themselves with the study of the teaching. By this was meant that the essential impulse of the Hasidic movement was the rebellion of the "ignorant" mass, in many ways treated with contempt by the religious tradition, against this scale of values in which the scholar, the man devoted to the knowledge of the Torah, occupied the highest rung. The true aim of the movement is thereby understood as one toward the revolution of values, toward a new order of rank in which it is not the man who "knows" the Torah, but the man who lives in it, who realizes it in the simple unity of life that stands in the highest place; and the simple unity is, in fact, more often found in the *am-haaretz* than in the *lamdan*, the thoroughly learned. The root of this striving for a revolution of values was seen to lie in the change of the social structure in East European Jewry since it took place in just that time when Hasidism came into the world.

60

The kernel of truth in this conception is unmistakable. One cannot understand the enormous influence that Hasidism exercised on the masses of the people if one does not recognize the "democratic" strain in it, the tendency native to it to set in place of the existing "aristocracy" of spiritual possession the equal right of all to draw near to the absolute Being. Inequality might rule in all matters of external life: in the innermost realm, in the relation to God it may not penetrate. From this standpoint it is easier to bear the reality of the distinction between the privileged and the unprivileged since the worst special privilege has been done away with. Certainly such a transformation can only take place in the history of religions when it has been preceded by convulsions in the inner core of the community; but the essential question is how great is the share of the social factor in this general process.

Since the significance of the social factor in the history of the spirit was discovered, one has naturally been inclined to give it undue weight. The main task here, in contrast, as in every genuine inquiry, is the demarcation of the spheres. But the limits of the power of the social factor can nowhere else be so clearly designated as in the history of religion. It determines that new contents of teaching and of life forms, new dogmas and myths, new symbols and rituals shall at a certain time outgrow others and find entrance into the life of the people—their extent and their reverberation depend on the social factor; but not the content itself. The belief that religious forms arise ever again out of social "relationships" is an error capable of impoverishing the

61

world of the spirit. These relationships influence the sphere within which the forms hold force: only under certain social conditions can the new prepare its way. But the new itself arises from the contacts and conflicts in the heart of religion itself. The economic development supplies here only the fertilizing forces; the spirit supplies the forces of the seed.

This holds particularly for that sphere of religious life within which Hasidism is one of the great historic manifestations. One is accustomed to call this sphere mysticism; but for the sake of clarity it must be pointed out that what is in question here is not speculations detached from human experience, speculations, perhaps, about the relation between God and the world by means of divine emanations, but a teaching that is grounded in human experience and that is solely concerned with the happenings between man and God. To be sure, this teaching makes use of those speculations and it may be that it will always continue to use them, as Hasidism does; but only in order to bind them ever again to human existence and the personal task of man, in order to authenticate them in existence and task. Mysticism in this sense points to the sphere of the person and builds on it, even though in its extreme forms it proclaims as its final goal the dissolution of the person, his merging into divine being. This is not to be understood, however, as if one had to concern oneself with this mysticism just in its isolation, because it is "personal." The mystic enters the room of his mystical experience, which is destined to become the foundation of his teaching, not from a neutral world-space but from the life-space of a concrete religion in which he is at home and to which he ever again returns home; indeed, even his experience itself is in no small measure stamped by the traditions and ordinances of this religion. Even if he seems to renounce the dogmas of his religion, he remains bound with its vitality. Mysticism is a historical phenomenon. It comes forward most strongly where it becomes a "movement," that is, where the teaching and the manner of teaching of the mystic takes effect outside the circle of his disciples, seizes the people, gives it example and model and calls forth profound transformations in the faith and the soul of the people.

If we ask now about the character of the historical situation in which the spark of mystical existence leaps over into the people, then we find for the most part that it is a time of a more or less public inner crisis of the religion. If the validity and reality of faith of the traditional contents and structures of a religion are shaken, whether because of an increasing degeneration or because of an extraordinary event, if, therefore, the response of this religion to the problematic of human existence, the existence of the individual and the existence of the people, becomes questionable, then mysticism not infrequently rises up against the spreading doubt, against the breaking out of despair. It remolds the basic motif of mystical speculation into life motifs, not merely in the presentations of the teaching, but above all in life itself, on the soil of the religious context from which it arose, and thus leads this religion to a fullness of new life-force. It strengthens the shaken structures, it dispenses new content to the statements that have become questionable and makes them worthy of belief, it pours a new meaning into the forms emptied of their meaning and renews them from within, it restores to religion its binding power. The fact that the people accept mysticism to such an extent is conditioned by social motives, by social changes, by social strivings, but what mysticism gives to the people is not understandable from the standpoint of the soil; the life-force that it presents to religion has its source in the inner religious dynamic itself, the formative sap in it ascends from those root beds in which the substance of faith decomposes and renews itself.

So it is with Hasidism.

II  The second part of the Sabbatian-Frankist revolt, the Satyr-drama, was bitterer than the first, the tragedy. This revolt did not merely bring Judaism to the rim of the abyss, as is usually said, but caused it already to lift one foot into the yawning gorge. That the central band of the possessed actually completed the change of faith, in the former case to Islam, secretly and under compulsion, in the latter to Christianity, openly and ostentatiously, but in both cases while elevating the event, as it were, into holy action in the service of the God of Israel—that this took place was only a symptom of the poisoning that had penetrated into the heart of the folk body. One may not regard the awesome process that extends over a century as an external catastrophe alone, from which base those especially affected remove themselves to outside the camp while the rest—those who were only partially seized by the convulsion—return into the accustomed path of their lives at more or less the same point. The seeds of disintegration have penetrated, without its having been noticed, into the most distant limbs of the people, those who had seemingly not been touched by the event, and even he who fiercely fought the evil must withstand its assault in the dark depths of his own soul, in the turmoil of dreams. Consequently, though every part of the folk body in which the pestilence had erupted in boils should be cut off from the whole, this would not bring about a healing: the powerful poison can only be overcome through a powerful antidote. What is of crucial importance is whether this antidote has already been prepared and kept ready in the innermost tissue of the organism so that it only needs to be developed and activated to its full strength and whether the developing and acting strength is at hand in the shape of a new leader, a new leadership. If these two conjoin, then the healing will succeed.

That poison cannot, like a chemical one, be designated with a name or a formula. If we wish to describe it indirectly, we can do so most easily if we speak of the lust for overrunning reality. Instead of making reality the starting point of life, reality that is full of cruel contradictions but just thereby calling forth true greatness, namely the quiet work of overcoming the contradictions, one surrenders to illusion, intoxicates oneself in it, subjugates life to it. In the same measure in which one does this, the core of his existence becomes burning and unfruitful at once, he becomes at once completely agitated and crippled in his motive power. This lust for overrunning reality leads, in addition, to one's acting and teaching as though a state of perfection, of Messianic fulfillment existed that does not in truth exist; it leads to an attitude that abolishes the structures and mutilates the values. It is thoroughly mistaken to speak here of an over-great zeal of faith: true faith, even the most zealous, is not "blind," it sees the reality and does not deceive itself; only it listens as well to what is above this reality, what commissions and empowers it to change reality. But if an illusory world is set in the place of the actual world, then superstition reigns, fraught with deadly peril.

This powerful poison too could only be conquered by a powerful antidote, and with an individual or a people who have surrendered themselves to illusion that can only take place through a renewed relationship to reality. "Renewed" means here, to be sure, a contrast to "old," for it is a vain effort to wish to bring about this relationship on the basis of earlier conditions instead of on the basis of those in which one finds oneself. One can seek the salvation for a historical hour only from its own presuppositions, which have never before been present. But it also means something other than "new," for the material needed for the production of the remedy cannot itself be produced, it must be already prepared. What matters is the reunification with the past and the revolution in one; the re-entrance into the tradition, but a tradition that has been transformed. It is this that took place here, in Hasidism. The renewed relationship to reality founded by it it mixed out of streams gushing forth, open and hidden ones; but what it drew from these has in its hands become new.

It has been a remedy; but that is not to be understood as if it arose out of an *intention* of healing. Remedies of this kind, that work in the breadth and in the depth, never arise out of a mere intention; they are the product of a personal *existence,* in which the salvation, the renewed relationship to reality, embodies itself. The existence is not directed to this working, it is only just what it is and therefore it works as it works. And certainly it interprets itself in a teaching, as one interprets a traditional text, but it does not thereby intend itself, rather the truth. Both together, the existence and the teaching that interprets it, make the medicine effective. They awaken a trust that is no longer fed by illusion but by reality, a trust in men and then in life, and then in God.

The personal existence that works with such effectiveness can only be a "naïve" one, that is, an existence that is wholly directed toward its object; it cannot be a "reflexive" one, that is one that occupies itself with its own problem. But it also cannot be a theoretical one, that is, one that wishes to comprehend the object toward which it is directed through seeking to abstract from the reality or to penetrate behind the reality as does the contemplative mystic. It can only be a vital

67

existence that lives directly with reality and in this simple life with reality thinks what it thinks and regards what it regards: no more and no less than what the concreteness of this life offers it. This naïveté, vitality, simplicity, and immediacy form the personal core around which the foundations of the new movement are laid. It works as a model of the renewed relationship to reality. It attracts all those of a kindred nature among the common people. It establishes the new type of leader. The appearance of the Baal-Shem-Tov is the founding fact of Hasidism.

In our time, which is quite passionately striving to wear away the personal form, it is customary to probe such appearances until as little as possible is left of the personal substance. Thus there is a tendency to set in the place of that first one, who is dear to tradition, disciples who, in contrast to him, have left behind a coherent doctrine. The interpretation that sees in Sabbatai Zvi only an instrument, unimportant in itself, that through highly gifted adherents is filled with personal content, as it were, and has been placed thus before a mass that is easily taken in, may, of course, be justified: in the realm of illusion such an inflation of nothing passes for central majesty. If, in contrast, one tries to shrink the figure of the Baal-Shem-Tov to a propagandistic embellishment that the great figures of Hasidic thought, allegedly the true founders of the movement, together with their disciples, have created, then one radically mistakes the nature of a movement of this kind. It begins with the relationship of a small community to a leading and teaching man; the *reality*

of this man and not his appearance is what constitutes
the community; from here ascends in ever-widening
circles the renewed relationship of the people to reality.
For as the individual, so also the totality can only win
a true relationship to reality through the relationship to
reality of a man: the world of illusion vanishes, being
itself becomes open, and one may trust it.

Even though the reliable information about the life
of the Baal-Shem-Tov is only limited, we possess a
faithful tradition that tells us that men of a high
spiritual rank, great men of the revealed and of the
secret teaching, paid him reverence and served him.
What the legend tells, that one man received from him
the solution of the most difficult problems when he
listened to his prayer, that a second man during the
prayer of the Baal-Shem-Tov broke out in a weeping
with which a complete transformation of his life com-
menced, that the spiritual power of a third disappeared
when he heard his simple words and he subjected
himself entirely to the wonderful man—all this is confirmed in its essentials through the accounts of his disciples themselves. The writings of one of them, Jacob
Joseph of Polnoy, whom we may call the Xenophon of
the Baal-Shem-Tov (he did not have a Plato, the one
who was capable of being that, Dov Baer, the Maggid
of Mezritsh, introduced into his discourses, to be sure,
some sayings of the master, but he said almost nothing
about his person), are a powerful testimony of the ven-
eration that the scholar cherished for the man of direct
illumination, a testimony of the complete change of the
scale of values. It is no longer the sharp-witted man,

versed in religious knowledge, nor is it the secluded
ascetic devoted to contemplation, but the pure and
unified man who walks with God in the midst of the
world, who participates in the life of the people and
raises it to God who is now held up as the exemplary
man.

We can ourselves sense something of that effect
when we read the words of the Baal-Shem-Tov. We
posses of his teachings, certainly, only what his disciples quoted, fragments the majority of which have
certainly been altered in the rendering, mixed with
amplifications of the disciples so that at first it seems to
us hopeless to extract the voice of the master from the
confusion of voices surrounding it. Nevertheless, we
can succeed in doing so in a certain measure, and just
because there are so many and so varied transmitters:
we can, as it were, detach all the multiplicity and there
remains before us something simple and united—not
a greater, more coherent discourse, not even enough to
reconstruct such a discourse if some such should at one
time have existed, but in any case the word of a man,
a word with its own tone and its own life-meaning. We
listen, listen, and then a surprising directness can be
perceived, that which only enters into the world of
speech when a man, after he has drained the goblet of
spiritual disappointments, dares to stand his ground before reality.

Only listen to a saying such as this which made me,
over forty years ago, into a Hasid of the Baal-Shem-
Tov: "He takes unto himself the quality of fervor. He
arises from sleep with fervor, for he is hallowed and

70

become another man and is worthy to create and is become like the Holy One, blessed be He, when He created His world." This saying rests, to be sure, upon several utterances of the Kabbalists; nevertheless, who before the Baal-Shem-Tov, who outside him has spoken to us thus? I say: to us, for this is what is decisive: he who has heard him feels as though his speech were addressed to him. The legend that tells how among the hearers of a discourse each had understood it as though it were spoken to him in answer to his need, his doubt, and the restless questioning of his innermost life—this legend certainly reports the truth. Just this truth we also perceive even now. It is not a teaching enclosed in itself, high above our existence, that transmits to our knowledge only a ray from the higher worlds, nor is it merely an instruction that shows our soul the path of ascent: it is a help for our concrete life—our life itself is uplifted through the speech directed to us if we listen to it. Reality calls forth reality; the reality of a man who has lived in intercourse with the reality of being in its fullness, awakens the reality in us and helps us to live in intercourse with the reality of being in its fullness. And here the words of the Baal-Shem-Tov as interpreted by Rabbi Jacob Joseph hold good: "If the disciples do not draw forth from the fountain, then the master is called heavy-tongued."

# III

The Sabbatian-Frankist crisis was before all a crisis of the teaching.

The Torah, the teaching of Israel, is a teaching of distinction. As the creation is founded on distinction: in space—between the higher and the lower waters, in time—between day and night and so forth, and at the end of creation stands man, he too divided into man and woman, so man is bidden by revelation to distinguish: between God and idols, between true and false prophets, between pure and impure, between good and evil, between sacred and profane; in sum, between that which conforms to God and that which does not conform to Him. There is no place for an indeterminate multiplicity, in everything the principle of polar duality rules. But in contrast to the cosmic divisions, which embrace both poles with the same affirmation, the divisions of revelation are either armed with the strongest accents of Yes and No, of pleasing to God and condemned by Him, as is the case with the "ethical" distinction between good and bad, or the perfection concentrates itself at the one end and leaves a wide room for all that is outside of it, as is the case with "cultic" distinction between sacred and profane. And the destiny of man, his destiny in the most exact sense of the term, that of the individual and that of the totality, depends upon the right distinction. In the sphere of the holy this finds expression in the tradition that whoever comes into unauthorized contact with its symbols has forfeited his life, in the realm of good and evil it finds expression in the message that God has placed before his people "life and good and death and evil." Here the structures of creation, to which life and death belong, are mixed with the structures of revelation. Thereby it becomes entirely clear at this point that the distinction that is taught in the Torah means decision, a decision in which man decides concerning himself.

But with the unfolding of the third realm, that is added to creation and revelation, the realm of the "end of days," the problem arises whether the distinction imposed upon men is valid forever. If a Messianic completion of creation is to be expected, a completion in which even man, and especially man, attains to his perfection, then there is no longer room in reality for the distinctions established in the Torah. If at the end of days, as the later prophets have envisioned it, the teaching will be inscribed in the hearts of men and they will know God directly, then along with the threat of sin the whole series of conceptions of crossroads and decisions will be abolished; the distinction between good and evil must then lose its concrete significance. Furthermore, if the task laid upon Israel, to become holy because its God is holy, attains to fulfillment in the time to come, then the distinction between holy and profane is thereby also abolished; for who becomes holy can then no longer do what was until then profane otherwise than in holiness; the whole realm of the profane is swallowed by the realm of the holy. In the Messianic perspective the essential distinctions of

73

the Torah appear provisional and temporary. What the perfected man does, what he lives, conforms, as such, with God. Of this man nothing more is demanded, he is free from all "ought"; for all that should be is here already done, man is as he is, he lives as he lives, and therein he has his perfection.

The Sabbatian movement, which found this view already fully present, concludes from the fact of the Messiah's having come that the presuppositions have already been fulfilled. It imagines—in the days of its origin doubtless with that measure of belief that is also given to the superstitions and later with the effort to attain to a similar state by way of a willed ecstasy— that the hour of completion is present. But it does not content itself with taking from the concept of sin its negative character and thus making sin into something neutral; it elevates it to holiness because it sees sin performed in holiness as preparing the way for the Messianic world. He who does in holiness what until then counted as sin conquers this piece of being for perfection. He penetrates into the "shell" and fills it with holiness until it bursts open. The work of redemption can only be completed when the redeeming force enters into the evil itself, overpowers it, transforms it, redeems it. That takes place through man doing evil without doing it as evil. There exists here, therefore, an antithesis between the action and the intention, but this antithesis is overcome through holiness: since this man is holy, all that he does is holy.

Such "gnostic" tendencies have arisen in the historical religions from time to time, and always rested on

74

the thesis that man has attained to his perfection and holiness in the form of this or that person. Always this one thing lay at the root of them all, that the person upon whom the spirit descended appeared, in his own view and in that of others, transformed into the perfected man and that his inner abundance and confusion were transfigured by attributes from the sphere of holiness. In Judaism the Messianic pathos was added to this, the inspired belief in the dependence of the redemption of people and world on the man who appears as the perfected man, and on his deeds. Here, as a result, the problematic penetrates into the innermost life of the people.

The teaching of Israel is a teaching of distinction; from now on there was nothing more to distinguish. The teaching of Israel means the reciprocal harmonizing of the distinction good-evil and the distinction holy-profane; from now on the fire of the "holy" has consumed the substance of good and evil. We could see in this a victory of the religious over the ethical if it did not rest on an illusion: with the exposure of the illusion the apparently victorious religious principle must relinquish the ground without the defeated ethical principle again coming into its own.

The crisis of the Torah was already at hand in latent form in the fact of the illusion; it broke out, as soon as this illusion had been seen through. To be sure, for many men the Torah remained in its place even then, as if nothing had happened; but its word no longer possessed any soul-compelling force. The persisting core of the people was shattered in its reality of faith.

75

That the Messianic hope has been denied does not yet
in itself bring with it any inner catastrophe; disappointed, exhausted, undermined, the people still turn
back to their unmessianic way of life, and the traditional structures help man to live his life. Not so if these
structures themselves are put in question. The Jewish
people had withstood the suffering of exile because it
was certain that in the Torah it possessed the right
way, a way that, even though the people might at times
fall away from it, still brings it to where it should go—
if one only knows how to distinguish between the right
way and the false ways. This knowledge seemed to be
taken from it in the days of illusion when one acted as
though one had attained the goal and a way was no
longer needed. The Torah had restrained and selec-
tively confronted the life of the impulses; it had bidden
man to remain near to the holy even in the natural
sphere of the profane. But now it seemed as if the holiness itself broke through all limits and established itself in the midst of the forbidden, in the impure. The
original illusion was indeed dispersed, that which deluded those who were possessed by it into believing
that the days of the Messiah had come, the Torah was
abolished and in its place had stepped the immediate
enjoyment of the divine in all things. But now there
arose, first, subtle helping constructions and after them
there came a new, now wholly unrestrained illusion.
Even he who combated it was touched by it in the
hidden corners of his soul. In the external world the
intoxication only seized the circle of sectarians; but in
secrecy the minds of men succumbed to it. The soul

whose bonds were loosed made bold to find God as its property in nature, in its own nature. It refused to return into the pre-Messianic age. And if men could no longer believe in perfection being at hand, then they conjured it up with all kinds of arts.

These are the days in which one still fulfills the commandments, but with a soul squinting away from its own acts. These are the days in which the evil prevails that the Torah has in mind: the penetration of chaos into the cosmos of revelation. These are the days of temptations, which the Torah in the heart is no longer strong enough to exorcise, for behind the demonic mask one imagines that the countenance of divine freedom is to be discovered; one does not let oneself be deluded by the temptations, but one also does not drive them out. They are particularly importunate during prayer; there every image becomes a temptation. They behave themselves as though they were at home and promise man another God than Him to whom he calls. The realms are overturned, everything encroaches on everything else, and possibility is more powerful than reality.

It was necessary that the teaching of the Baal-Shem commence at this point and bring healing, and it did so.

IV        Legend tells that in the days of the Baal-Shem-Tov there was a man who was famous for the wonderful qualities of his spirit. The Hasidim asked their master whether it would be proper for them to go to that man and test him. "Go then," he said. Again they asked him: "How shall we know whether he is a real zaddik?"

"Ask of him advice," answered the Baal-Shem-Tov, "as to how the 'alien thoughts' are to be expelled. If he gives you such advice, then you will know that he is of no importance. For with this a man must struggle until his last moment, and just that is the service of man in the world." The alien thoughts that accost man in the hours of prayer and study in order to divert his mind and to seduce him so that he desires the things that rise before his inner eye—their determining power in the course of life is great, and we may not wish that they should wholly leave us. In our language: the fantasy—for it is of this that we are speaking—that wishes to draw us away from the truth is a necessary element in its service. We should not thrust away its abundance that waylays our hearts, but receive it and fit it into real existence; only in the strength of such an act shall we attain to that unity that does not look away from the world but embraces it. But to do this we must accomplish what is hardest of all: the transformation. We must transform the element that wants to take possession of us into the substance of true life.

To understand this aright, we must above all grasp something essential: the "alien thoughts"—their coming to man and their working on him—are not, in the eyes of the Baal-Shem-Tov, what we call a psychological phenomenon, but a phenomenon that belongs to the cosmic sphere and even extends beyond it. In each of them dwells a spark, that stems from the primordial revolution of the upper worlds, from the "Breaking of the Vessels," in the language of the Kabbala. They are "clear lights," "that have sunk into the depths and have taken on soiled clothing." From this, its prison, the spark is anxious to be delivered, and this, its anxiety, is the driving force that brings the "alien thoughts" to man. If he succeeds in liberating the pure spark from the demonic "shells," then he helps it return to its divine origin. So the Baal-Shem-Tov interprets the Biblical verse bidding the beautiful woman, whom a man in her captivity saw, desired, and took to wife: "She shall cast off from herself the garment of her captivity." One shall not accept the alien thought as it appears, in its defiled clothing, but one shall cast off its clothing, then its light will arise like the flush of dawn. In reality it is the divine being itself that hides in the "alien thoughts" and wants one to discover it therein, to break through to it and liberate it; God Himself approaches us and demands of us.

What we describe as imagination is therefore no free play of the soul but a real meeting with real elements of being that are outside of us, and what matters is not to surrender to the images of fantasy that appear, but to separate the kernel from the shell and to redeem those elements themselves. What we suppose we effect merely in our souls, in reality we effect on the destiny of the world. He who does not believe that does not fully take on himself "the yoke of the kingdom of heaven," for he curtails the reality of God. He who fully takes on himself the yoke of the kingdom of heaven, knows each time: "Not for nothing has this thought come to me, but that I might raise it, and if not now, when?"

From this standpoint we gain an insight into the relation between good and evil, which is thoroughly different from the usual merely-ethical viewpoint. In this insight the teaching of the Talmud that one must serve God with both urges, that is, allow all the force that breaks forth in desire to flow into service, is fused with the Kabbala's teaching of the fallen sparks. The Shekina embraces both, the "good" and the "evil," but the evil not as an independent substance, rather as the "throne of the good," as "the lowest rung of the fully good," as the power that leads astray and that only needs the direction to God in order to become "good." It is the thornbush which, seized by divine fire, becomes the revelation of God.

The evil urge "disguises itself as a servant who revolts against his master"; but in reality he is faithful and fulfills his task. All temptations come from God who clothes Himself in the "evil" forces. But they are real temptations: the fateful seriousness of the choice, the pathos of the ever-recurring partings of the way into life and death are in the thoughts of the Baal-Shem no less marked than in any other age, only evil and good are no longer sundered from one another like two different qualities but like the unformed and the formed material, no longer like left and right, but like above and below, like thornbush and fire. Man must let the thornbush be entirely penetrated by the fire. He must join to God the desire of the temptation itself.

He must so uplift the love for a beautiful creature that it becomes love for the Source of all beauty, the Source that makes the beautiful beautiful: thus love returns home from exile. He must uplift the fear that seizes him before a human or cosmic might into fear before the might of the Almighty, the fear that has clothed itself in that human or cosmic might: thereupon the fear persists no longer as dread but as wonder and reverence. He must forge the glowing mass of wrath into zeal for God. He must transform the pleasures of earth into the enjoyment of heavenly splendor.

Sin is the going astray of the force, but the force that goes astray is itself from God. "The Shekina is from above to below, to the end of all rungs, and this is the mystery of the saying, 'And Thou dost animate them all.' Even when a man commits a sin, the Shekina clothes itself in it. For if this were not so, there would be in him no strength to act and to move a limb . . . And this is, as it were, the exile of the Shekina." If we make use of the force of the Shekina to do evil, then we drive it itself into exile.

Since this is so, since sin is only the erring outbreak of a great force that comes from the Shekina, we can understand the mystery of the pleasure that the sinner experiences, but also the mystery of the turning. For he who has sinned is not yet lost. Though you have cast off the sparks through your sin, you have not yet barred their ascent: it is within your power to raise them through your turning. That is what is meant when it is said of God that He "bears falling away": he bears and raises it into the upper world. Therefore, the wicked

81

man who is full of desire and is able to turn is dearer
to God than the seemingly righteous man who fulfills
all external commandments without true devotion of
the heart, without the "cleaving," and before whom,
since he regards himself as welcome, the gates of the
turning are barred. But also among the genuinely
righteous there are two kinds. One recognizes them
by their relation to the evil urge. The one acts like a
man who notices at night that a thief has crept into his
store and cries out: the thief flees and all is as if nothing
had happened. The other is like one who does not
alarm the thief but lets him draw near until he can lay
hold of him and bind him. The first drives away the
evil, the second transforms it into good; and it is to this
latter that the saying applies: "Who is a hero? He who
masters his urges." He compels the evil urge to teach
him, and he learns from it. The verse of the Bible,
"From every man whose heart stirs him, shall you take
my offering," the Baal-Shem interprets thus: Every
man recognizes and grasps the quality with which he
must serve God by that for which he longs.

This is the one antidote that Hasidism produced.
Sabbatianism had created the illusion that one could
redeem evil by doing it without intending it as evil.
That is an illusion, for all that man does reacts on his
soul, even when he imagines that his soul floats above
the deed. In opposition to this, Hasidism has established the fact that one can give the directionless force
that breaks out in the desire the direction to the truth,
that one can make the blind force see. Thereby the
teaching of the distinction is renewed in a time in

which the distinction between good and evil had become questionable.

The psychoanalysis of our day has taken up the Hasidic view anew in the form of the theory of "sublimating the libido." According to this theory one can divert the impulse from its immediate object and transfer it to the realm of the spirit, therefore, as it were, changing its energy form. Everything is here limited to psychic events alone, in contrast to which Hasidism teaches ever again the real contact with other beings. "Sublimation" takes place within man, the "raising of the sparks" takes place between man and the world.

V    That the essence of the Hasidic message consists in founding a renewed relation to reality becomes still more evident in another basic viewpoint that is linked with the first but extends beyond the sphere of the soul in further measure than it.

The sparks teaching of the later Kabbala became an ethical teaching in the hands of the Baal-Shem-Tov and expanded to a task that embraced the whole life of man. In the primordial time of being, in the time when God built worlds and tore them down, sparks have fallen into all things of the world. In a material shell, in a mineral, in a plant, in an animal the spark is hidden, a complete figure like that of a man, doubled up, his head on his thighs without being able to move his hands and feet, like an embryo. Only through man is there a redemption for him. It is up to man to purify the sparks out of the things and beings that he meets day by day, and raise them to ever higher rungs, to ever higher births, from mineral to plant, from plant to animal, from animal to man until the holy spark can return to its origin. If you accomplish this, it is as if you had liberated a king's son from captivity.

Man's service of the sparks takes place in everyday life; men can accomplish it even with the most profane bodily action that brings him into contact with things and beings, for even the most profane action can be done in holiness, and he who does it in holiness raises the sparks. In the clothes that you wear, in the tools that you use, in the food that you eat, in the domestic animal that toils for you, in all are hidden sparks that are anxious for redemption, and if you have to do with the things and beings with carefulness, with good will, and faithfulness, you redeem them. God gives you the clothes and food that belong to the roots of your soul in order that you may redeem the sparks in them. One can serve Him with all actions, and He wills that one serve Him with all. Therefore it says, "On all your ways shalt thou know Him." As the seed sown in the ground draws its strength from it and from it makes the fruit, so the man, who fulfills the service draws the sparks from all the things that belong to the root of his soul and raises them to God.

The disciples frequently quote the Baal-Shem-Tov's interpretation of the wonderful Aggadic saying that tells of the patriarch Enoch that he was a cobbler, and with every stitch of his awl, as it sewed together the upper leather and the sole, he joined together God and His Shekina. The Baal-Shem-Tov quoted the verse of the Bible, "All that thy hand finds to do, do in thy strength." All that you do, so the Baal-Shem-Tov interpreted it, do it with the strength of your soul and of your thoughts that you may join the Holy One, praised be He, with His Shekina. By this two things are said. First, all that man does he shall do with his whole being. And to preclude the view that spiritual values alone are meant thereby, the Baal-Shem-Tov explicitly says: "That he does the deed that he does with all his limbs." What is involved, therefore, is the whole spiritual-physical being, that comes to perfect unity through the diffusion of the spirit in all limbs; with this united spiritual-physical being, with this united strength, man shall do what he does.

Second, it is incumbent upon man to do all that he does with his intention directed to the unification of the highest divine being with its Shekina, which dwells in the world. But nowhere here, in contrast to all ascetic teaching that strives to surmount reality, is it intimated that the indwelling principle would draw itself out of the world; rather the unification of the separated means just the unification of God with the world, which continues to exist as world, only that it is now, just as world, redeemed. In each movement that he makes, in each word that he speaks, man shall direct his being to this unification, and the significance of this for concrete life is expressed by a disciple of a disciple of the Baal-Shem-Tov in a clear example, undoubtedly in the spirit of the master: "In business his

mind is devoted to human beings with love and friendship." The same disciple concludes elsewhere the exposition of this teaching with words that lay especial
stress on its central importance: "For if you do not
believe that the reality of God is in all things, and you
can by means of everything that is in the world achieve
unifications, with all work and business and eating and
drinking, but you do not believe and do not do it, and
you regard it as evil and flee from it, then is there
necessarily (here comes the interpretation of the con-
tinuation of that verse from Ecclesiastes, "All that thy
hands find to do, do in thy strength") 'nothing,' for
the 'work and calculation and cleverness' that thou hast
'are in the netherworld to which thou goest.'"

The decisive step is thereby taken to the renewel of
the relation to reality. Only on the path of true intercourse with the things and beings does man attain to
true life, but only on this path can he take an active
part in the redemption of the world. The Baal-Shem-
Tov, as has been said, saw even in the power of imagination a kind of meeting for which there are special
tasks; more than ever, existence in reality is recognizable as an unbroken chain of meetings, each of which
demands the person for what can be fulfilled by him,
just by him and just in this hour. In opposition to the
illusion of ostensibly-attained perfection, as it prevailed
in the confusion of the false Messianic, here stands the
life of the everyday, which has found its fulfillment as
the true miracle.

And thereby the crisis of the Torah is overcome. The
teaching of the "alien thoughts," which transformed the

86

speculation of the Kabbala into a living and popular ethos, renewed the distinction between good and evil, but in such a way that it now entered into the problematics that had arisen in the epoch and answered it. It no longer contented itself with repelling evil as befitted pre-Sabbatian ages; it took into itself the new experience, the experience of the ravishment of sin, and affirmed the forces of the desire, indeed actually demanded them, in order to direct them to their true goal. The teaching of "Enoch the Cobbler" proceeded from that speculation, but it went further. As fundamental as the distinction between the holy and the profane was in Judaism, the wish still awoke ever again to invest the holy with effect and influence in the realm of the profane and so build the bridge. This wish now entered into fulfillment. Nothing in the world is entirely alien to the holy, anything can become its vessel. The Sabbatian theology preached the conquest of sin through the holy; now the demonic character of this preaching is revealed by the simple Hasidic commandment that entered into the heart of the simple man of faith, the commandment to do all that one does with one's whole being. For sin is just that which by its nature one cannot do with the whole being: it is possible to silence the contradiction in the soul, but it is not possible to extirpate it. Now, in the teaching of the Baal-Shem-Tov, in contrast, the conquest of the realm of the profane by the holy, the conquest of the realm of permissible things, of the adiaphora, genuinely ensues. There sin was pronounced holy; here what is

87

called for is to hallow the intercourse with all things and beings in the life of the everyday.

The first revolt of the *am-haaretz*, the movement of early Christianity, stormed out of the gates of Judaism. Its second revolt, the Hasidic, remained within the borders of Israel. For, in distinction to the first which demanded that one should live as though the Kingdom of God had already dawned, Hasidism affirmed the natural reality of the still unmessianic hour as the material to be hallowed, and thereby it also affirmed the people as such, the great unholy body, which is destined to be hallowed.

# CHAPTER III

# SPINOZA,
# SABBATAI ZVI,
# AND THE BAAL-SHEM

**I**        Thirty-two years before the Baal-Shem-Tov was born, there died within a short space of time two remarkable Jews. Both no longer belonged to the Jewish community, the one, the philosopher Baruch Spinoza, through the excommunication of the synagogue, the other, the "Messiah" Sabbatai Zvi, through conversion to Islam. These two men mark a late-exilic catastrophe of Judaism, Spinoza a catastrophe in spirit and in the influence on the Gentile nations, Sabbatai Zvi in life and in the inner structure. Spinoza has certainly remained without important historical influence on Judaism, but still he belongs in its course of history, and in an essential manner; for as Sabbatai's apostasy signified the historical placing in question of Jewish Messianism, so Spinoza's teaching signified the historical placing in question of the Jewish belief in God. Both thereby conducted to its conclusion a process which had begun with a single historical manifestation, with Jesus. To both a new process provided the reply and the correction, a process which also began with a single historical manifestation, with that of the Baal-Shem-Tov.

The great deed of Israel is not that it taught the one real God, who is the origin and goal of all being, but that it pointed out that this God can be addressed by man in reality, that man can say Thou to Him, that he can stand face to face with Him, that he can have intercourse with Him. Wherever there is man, to be sure, there is also prayer, and so it has probably always been. But only Israel has understood, or rather actually lives, life as being addressed and answering, addressing and receiving answer. Mystery cults at all stages of mankind, to be sure, have wanted to introduce man into an apparently much more intimate interchange with the deity; but, as everywhere where it is a question of an exceptional state of being instead of the lived everyday, in what is felt here as the divine only an image born of man is to be perceived, an image of a partial manifestation of the real God who is the goal and origin of all being.

> The little finger of His left hand
> Is named Pan.

God in all concreteness as speaker, the creation as speech: God's call into nothing and the answer of things through their coming into existence, the speech of creation enduring in the life of all creation, the life of each creature as dialogue, the world as word—to proclaim this Israel existed. It taught, it showed that

91

the real God is the God who can be addressed because he is the God who addresses.

Jesus—not, certainly, the actual man Jesus, but the image of Jesus as it entered into the soul of the peoples and transformed it—allows God to be addressed only in conjunction with himself, the Christ. Only as borne along by him, the Logos, can the human word now penetrate to Him who is the origin and goal of all being; the "way" to the Father now goes only through him. In this modified form the peoples received Israel's teaching that God can be addressed. It came to pass that they learned to address Christ in His place.

Spinoza undertook to take from God His being open to man's address. One cannot suppose that his *deus sive natura* is "another God." He himself meant no other than Him whom he had addressed as a boy, Him who is the very origin and goal of all being; he only wanted to purify Him from the stain of being open to address. A God who was capable of being addressed was not pure enough, not great enough, not divine enough for him. The fundamental error of Spinoza was that he imagined that in the teaching of Israel only the teaching that God is a person was to be found and he opposed it as a diminution of divinity. But the truth of the teaching is that God is *also* a person, and this is, in contrast to all impersonal, unaddressable "purity" of God, an augmentation of divinity. Solomon, who built the Temple, knew that the whole of the heavens do not reach God and that He nonetheless elects for Himself a dwelling in the midst of those who address Him, that He is therefore both, the boundless and nameless as well as the father who teaches His children to address Him. Spinoza knew only: person or not person. He overthrew person as an idol and proclaimed the substance existing from itself to whom it would be folly or bad poetry to say Thou.

However little late-exilic Judaism learned from Spinoza, through him something of Judaism entered into the possession of the peoples, and what entered thus cannot be cut off from its origin. Something from the innermost center of Israel, however modified, had once penetrated through Christianity into the Gentile world. It is of great significance that only a Jew could teach men how to do away with it, and a Jew has done so. Spinoza helped the mind of the intellectual among the peoples to liberate itself from that which had penetrated it; the tendency of the Western spirit toward monological life was decisively forwarded by him —and thereby the crisis of the spirit in general since in the air of monological life it must gloriously wither.

The Baal-Shem-Tov probably knew nothing of Spinoza; nevertheless he has given the reply to him. In the truth of history one can reply without having heard; he does not mean what he says as a reply, but it is one. And that the reply of the Baal-Shem did not come to the attention of the spirits who received the speech of Spinoza, also does not diminish its significance; in the truth of history even what remains unknown can be valid.

In order to make clear this first character of reply of the Hasidic message, I must indicate a basic theme of Spinoza's that is closely bound up with that of the "purification" of God, but seems to belong to a still deeper level of the spirit.

The real communion of man wtih God not only has its place in the world, but also its subject. God speaks to man in the things and beings that He sends him in life; man answers through his action in relation to just these things and beings. All specific service of God has its meaning only in the ever-renewed preparation and hallowing for this communion with God in the world. But there is a danger, in fact, the utmost danger and temptation of man, that something becomes detached from the human side of this communion and makes itself independent, rounds itself off, seemingly perfects itself to reciprocity, yet puts itself in the place of real communion. The primal danger of man is "religion."

That which thus makes itself independent can be the forms in which man hallows the world for God, the "cultic-sacramental." Now they no longer mean the consecration of the lived everyday, but its amputation; life in the world and the service of God run side by side without connection. But the "God" of this service is no longer God; it is the semblance—the real partner of the communion is no longer there; the gestures of intercourse fall on the empty air.

Or it may be the state of the soul accompanying the communion that makes itself independent, the devotion, the intention, the absorption, the ecstasy. What was destined and directed to flow into confirmation in the fullness of life is cut off from that fullness. The soul wants to have to do with God alone, as if God wished that one exercise one's love for Him toward

Him alone and not toward His world. Now the soul imagines that the world has disappeared from between it and God, but with the world, God Himself has disappeared; only it alone, the soul, is there. What it calls God is only an image within it, what it conducts as dialogue is a monologue with divided roles; the real partner of communion is no longer there.

Spinoza lived in an age in which the becoming independent of soul and cult once again combined. Having become aware of its alienation from God, the West did not seek to give its world-life the direction to God, but to enter into a world-free intercourse with God in mystical and sacramental exaltation. The charming fictitiousness of Baroque is the artistic issue of this undertaking. From Spinoza's spiritual attitude it can be seen that such would-be intercourse was what he really held to be impure. Not outside the world, but only in the world itself can man find the divine; Spinoza set this thesis in opposition to the bifurcation of life that had become current in his age. He did so out of a primal Jewish impulse; out of a similar impulse there once arose the protest of the prophets against the sacrificial cults which had become independent. But his attack swung beyond this legitimate object. Along with world-free intercourse, all personal intercourse with God became unworthy of belief for him. The insight that God cannot be addressed apart from the unreduced reality of life because just in it He speaks, was inverted for him into the view that there is no speech between God and man. From being the place of the meeting with God, the world becomes for him the place of God.

That the Hasidic message may be understood as a reply to Spinoza, even though its speakers and hearers knew nothing of him, arises from the fact that it expressed the confession of Israel in a new manner, one through which, in fact, it became a reply. From of old Israel confessed that the world is not the place of God, rather that God is "the place of the world," and that He still "dwells in" it. Hasidism expressed this primal proposition anew, namely in a wholly practical manner. Through God's indwelling in the world the world becomes—in general religious terms—a sacrament; it could not be such if it were the place of God: only just this, that God transcends it yet dwells in it makes it a sacrament.

This is no objective expression, which can rightly exist independent of the lived life of the human person, still less, to be sure, one which can be enclosed within the subjectivity of the person alone. In the concrete contact with man the world again and again becomes sacramental. That means: in the concrete contact of its things and beings with this man, you, me. The things and beings, in which all the divine sparks dwell, are entrusted to this man that he may redeem the sparks in his contact with them. That one has thus been given charge of the things and beings in their sacramental possibility—this constitutes the existence of man in the world. This world is not, therefore, like that of Spinoza, a world persevering beyond the life that is to be lived and the death that is to be died, mine and yours, but the concrete world of this moment of personal existence, ready to be a sacrament, ready to bear the real happening of redemption. It is that which is entrusted to us, that which is joined to us, that which is offered us; it is that in which God addresses me and in which He wants to receive an answer from me.

The self-enjoyment of the soul which confounds its entangled self-intercourse with true dialogue in the All-Light is here excluded; God is not indifferent to His creation. But also excluded is the metaphysical construction of the spirit that believes that it can gaze into Being through looking away from the lived situation and imagines that it can talk about God as though He sat as a model for its conceptual images. Such metaphysics misses the God who hides Himself rather in the irreducible particulars of just this moment of thought, a mystery not to be delineated by any concept, yet appearing, addressing, offering itself in the concreteness of the situation—and rejected without answer in metaphysical looking-away.

In this basic attitude, the factual receiving of God in the things, the Hasidic message is a completion and extension of the ancient teaching of Israel. A completion: "Be holy, for I am holy" shows itself in the whole realm of the law not as a command for the hallowing of man away from the things, but for the hallowing of things through man, as his service to creation. But at the same time an extension. Thus the sacrifice in ancient Israel is the cultic sister of the meal that cannot exist without it, thereby hallowing part of just the same organic material the rest of which fell to the nourishment of men. But in Hasidic life eating itself has become sacramental service: through the hallowed receiving of food there takes place for animals and plants the redemption of the creature through the up-lifting of the sparks. If the distinction of the law be-tween pure and impure animals still sets to work here, limiting and circumscribing, so in the extension of the hallowing to all activities, the setting apart of the province of nature fundamentally removed from hal-lowing is fundamentally overcome: all that is allotted to the human person for his use, from cow and tree to field and tool, conceals sparks that want to be uplifted through this man, that will be uplifted by this man in holy use; and even meetings with strange things and beings in foreign lands means a holy deed.

But it is not merely in the world that there is no longer a basic division: also in the soul of man. As the things and beings which one has to work with have been entrusted to him, so also the apparently strange conceptions, thoughts, wishes that fall into the soul. In all of them vibrate sparks that want to be redeemed by man. Nothing, in fact, is unholy in itself, nothing is in itself evil. What we call evil is only the directionless plunging and storming of the sparks in need of redemp-tion. It is "passion"—the very same power which, when it has been endowed with direction, the one direction, brings forth the good in truth, the true service, the hallowing. Thus there no longer exist side by side in the soul of man the worldly and the spiritual, qualitatively sundered, there is now only power and direction. He who divides his life between God and the world, through giving the world "what is its" to save for God "what is His," denies God the service He demands, the giving of direction to all power, the hallowing of the everyday in the world and the soul.

In the Hasidic message the separation between "life in God" and "life in the world," the primal evil of all "religion," is overcome in genuine, concrete unity. But a rejoinder is also given here to the false overcoming of the separation through the abstract dissolution of the difference between God and the world. Hasidism preserves undiminished God's distance from and superiority to the world in which He nonetheless dwells. In this distance Hasidism sets the undivided wholeness of human life in its full meaning: that it should receive the world from God and act on the world for the sake of God. Bound to the world, receiving and acting, man stands directly before God—not "man" rather, but this particular man, you, I.

This very teaching of man's being bound with the world in the sight of God, the reply of Hasidism to Spinoza, was the one element through which Hasidism so overpoweringly entered into my life. I early had a premonition, indeed, no matter how I resisted it, that I was inescapably destined to love the world.

**II** And the other element—yet basically it is no other, but the same.

What is the meaning of the world's need for redemption? But what is the meaning of the indwelling of God, "He who dwells with them in the midst of their uncleanness"? It is basically the same question. The uncleanness of creation and its need for redemption are one; that God dwells in it and that God wills to redeem it, these too are one.

The uncleanness of creation and not merely of man; the indwelling of God in the world and not merely in the soul; one must proceed from here to grasp what the Hasidic message has to say concerning redemption.

What we call "evil" is not merely in man; it is in the world as the bad; it is the uncleanness of creation. But this uncleanness is not a nature, not an existent property of things. It is only its not standing firm, not finding direction, not deciding.

God has created a world and has called what was created very good—where then does the bad come from? God has created a world and has celebrated its completion—where then does the incomplete come from?

The gnosis of all ages opposes to the good power of God another primal power that works evil; it wishes history to be viewed as the battle between these two powers and the redemption of the world as the victorious consummation of this battle. But we know what has been proclaimed by the anonymous prophet whose words stand in the second part of the Book of Isaiah: that like light and darkness, so good and evil have been created by God Himself. No uncreated power stands in opposition to him.

Then is not the evil, the bad, a nature, an existent

property, after all? But the darkness also is no nature, but the abyss of the absence of light and the struggle for light; and even as such created by God.

The Bible sees evil as penetrating into creation through a deed of the first men; but it knows a non-human creature who insinuates just this deed and is therefore evil, the "serpent." Late Kabbalistic teaching, within the framework of which Hasidism developed, removes the penetration of evil back into the event of creation itself. The fire-stream of creative grace pours itself out in its fullness over the first-created primal shapes, the "vessels"; but they do not withstand it, they "break in pieces"—the stream showers an infinity of "sparks," the "shells" grow around them, the lack, the uncleanness, the evil has come into the world. Now the incomplete cleaves to the completed creation; a suffering world, a world in need of redemption lies at God's feet. But He does not leave it to lie in the abyss of its strugglings; after the sparks of His creative fire fall into the things, His glory itself descends to the world, enters into it, into "exile," dwells in it, dwells with the troubled, the suffering creatures in the midst of their uncleanness—desiring to redeem them.

If the Kabbala does not say so explicitly, still it unmistakably includes in this teaching the conception that already these primal vessels, like the first men, were accorded a movement of their own, an independence and freedom, if it was only the freedom to stand firm in the face of the stream of grace or not to stand firm. The sin of the first men is also, in fact, represented as a not standing firm: all is granted to them,

101

the whole fullness of grace, even the tree of life is not forbidden them; only just the knowledge of limitation, of the relations of the original purity and the uncleanness that has come to be in creation, only just the mystery of the primal lack, the mystery of "good and evil" God has reserved for Himself. But they did not stand firm before the fullness; they followed the promptings of the element of limitation. It is not as if they revolted against God; they do not decide against Him, only they just do not decide for Him. It is no rebellious movement; it is a perplexed, directionless, "weak-minded," indolent movement, this "stretching out of the hand." They do not do it, they have done it. One sees in them the directionless storming and plunging of the sparks in need of redemption—temptation, turmoil, and undecided deed. And so they "know" the limited, of course, just as man, as men know, as Adam later "knew" his wife; they know the limited, mixing themselves with it, knowing "good-and-evil," taking this good-and-evil into themselves, like plucked and eaten fruit.

A not standing firm, therefore—we know it, we for whom day after day the situation of the first men ever again recurs for the first time; we know this suffering action that is nothing but a reaching out from the directionless whirl; we know about the storming and plunging and self-entangling of the sparks, we know that what moves them is our badness, our need and desire for redemption. And perhaps we know too the other, those mysterious, inconceivable moments, that gentlest breakthrough, the receiving of direction, the decision,

102

the turning of the swirling world-movement to God.
Here we experience directly that self-movement, independence, freedom is accorded us. Whatever may be
the case with the rest of creation apart from man, we
know of man that in being created he has been set in
life as one who, in reality and not in fleeting moments
of self-deception, can do two things: choose God and
reject God. His ability to fall signifies his ability to
ascend; that he can bring ruin on the world signifies
that he can work for its redemption.

However narrowly some religions and theologies
may wish to understand it (perhaps as the mere capacity to believe or to refuse belief), this concrete
receiving of man into power remains the real core of
the religious life because it is just the core of human
life in general. However narrowly it has been understood, the fact remains that the creation of this creature
man signifies the mysterious saving-out of a codeter-
mining strength, a starting-point for events, a beginning. Not at one time only, but at all times does this
creature stand free to choose God or to reject Him, or
rather to leave unchosen. Does that mean that God has
given away a portion of his determining might? We
only ask that when we are busy subsuming God under
the laws of our logic. But the moment of breakthrough
in which we experience directly that we are free and
yet now know directly that God's hand has carried us,
teaches us from out of our own personal life to draw
near to the mystery in which man's freedom and God's
determining power, the reality of man and the reality
of God, are no longer contradictory.

103

One can also put the question otherwise. The first men stood in freedom before they fell away from God. Does that mean that God had not willed what they did? How then can something happen that God does not will? No theological argumentation can be of any further help to us here, only the determined insight that God's thoughts are not like our thoughts, that His will cannot be grasped and handled like ours. We may say that God wills that man should choose Him and not fall away from Him; but we must add to that that God wills that His creation not be an end in itself, that His world be a way. Further, in order that this take place in reality, the creature must of himself walk the way, of himself and ever again of himself: the fall must be as real as the redemption. Man is the creature in whom the path of the world is concentrated and represented. As of himself he completes the fall, so he must be able of himself really to work on redemption. Does that mean that God is not able to redeem His world without man's cooperation? It means that God wills not to be able. Does God need man for His work? He wills to need him.

God wills to need man for the work of completing His creation; in this sentence is to be grasped the foundation of the Jewish doctrine of redemption. But that God wills this means that this "needing" becomes working reality: in history as it takes place, God waits for man.

It is not merely in appearance that God has entered into exile in His indwelling in the world; it is not merely in appearance that in His indwelling He suffers

104

with the fate of His world. And it is not merely in appearance that He waits for the initial movement toward redemption to come from the world—really initiating and not merely in appearance. How it happens that this is not appearance but reality, how something from out of His world, whether it be falling away or returning, can happen to God, the All-powerful and the All-knowing, that is a mystery of God the Creator and Redeemer, not more mysterious to me than that He is; and that He is is to me almost less mysterious than that I am, I who write this with trembling fingers on a rock bench above a lake.

It would be senseless to ponder how great the share of man may be in the redemption of the world. No share of man and share of God exists. There is no "up to here" and "from there on"; there is nothing measurable and weighable here; basically, it would already be false to speak of a working together. That is true, indeed, for all human life and perhaps for all created life. It is senseless to ask how far my own action reaches and where God's grace begins; they do not in the least limit each other. Rather what alone concerns me before I bring something about is my action and what alone concerns me after it has been accomplished is God's grace; the latter not less really than the former, and neither of the two a partial cause. God and man do not divide the government of the world between them; man's effecting is enclosed in God's effecting and is still real effecting.

Thus the lived moment of man stands in truth between creation and redemption; it is joined to his being acted upon in creation, but also to his power to work for redemption. Rather he does not stand between the two but in both at once; for as creation does not merely take place once in the beginning but also at every moment throughout the whole of time, so redemption does not take place merely once at the end, but also at every moment throughout the whole of time. The moment is not merely joined to both, both are included in it. Creation did not "really" take place once for all, nor is it now merely "carried on," as it were, so that all acts of creation, including this one that now takes place, add up to the work of creation. Rather the word of the prayerbook, that God renews the work of creation every day, is entirely true. The act of creation that now takes place, is thus wholly capable of initiating, and the creative moment of God stands not only in the sequence of time, but in His own absoluteness. As in the realm of creation, in which God alone rules, the moment is thus not merely from somewhere, but occurs out of itself and in itself, so is it in the realm of redemption, in which God grants and demands that His effecting should incomprehensibly enclose the effecting of the human person. Not merely toward the goal of perfection, but in itself, too, the redemptive moment is real. Each one touches directly on the mystery of fulfillment; each not merely borne by the goal but also by meaning; each inserted in the sequence of time, inserted in its place in the great path of the world and there being effective, but each also sealed in its testimony. That does not mean that the moment becomes a mystical timeless now, rather that it is filled

106

with time: in the wavering fraction of time, the full-ness of time announces itself—not as a happening in the soul, but as a bodily happening in the world, out of the concrete meeting between God and man. It is "the down-flowing of the blessing."

The Hasidic message has also expressed in a quite practical way the knowledge, handed down to it in secret and open teachings, concerning this All-Day of redemption. And, in opposition to the enormous ap-paratus of Kabbalistic instructions, in opposition to the powerful exertions of "him who hastens the End," it has proclaimed in the strongest and clearest manner: there is no definite, exhibitable, teachable, magic ac-tion in established formulae and gestures, attitudes and tensions of the soul, that is effective for redemption; only the hallowing of all actions without distinction, only the bearing to God of ordinary life as it comes to pass and as it happens, only the consecration of the natural relationship with the world possesses redemp-tive power. Only out of the redemption of the everyday does the All-Day of redemption grow.

On this teaching the Hasidic reply to that catas-trophe of Jewish Messianism that stands under the name of Sabbatai Zvi is founded—a reply not merely in the truth of history, but also taking place in its reality.

It is a mistake to regard Jewish Messianism as a be-lief in an event happening once at the end of time and in a single human figure created as the center of this event. The assurance of the co-working strength that is accorded to man, to the generations of man, unites the end of time with the life lived in this present. Already in the prophecy of the first exile there appears a mysteriously strong intimation of the series of "servants of the Lord," arising from generation to generation, who lowly and despised, bear and purify the uncleanness of the world. In later writings this intimation is supplemented by a secret perspective of world history in which the great figures of Biblical narrative also bear a Messianic character: each of them was summoned, each refused to some extent; the special particular sin of each implied just that refusal before the Messianic summons. Thus God awaits in the generations of men the man in whom the indispensable movement from the side of the creature wins its decisive power. With the deepening of the exile of the world, which is represented by the exile of Israel, those servants who appear in each generation sink from the openness into the hiddenness; they no longer perform their deed in the light of known history, but in the darkness of an inaccessible personal work of suffering, of which no report or only a distorted one reaches the outer world. But the more sorrowful the fate of the world becomes, the fate with which God suffers through His indwelling in the world, so much the more does the life of this man become meaningful and effective in itself. They are no longer mere foreshadowings of the Messianic figure, as it were; rather in them the Messiahship of the end of time is preceded by one of all times, poured out over the ages, and without this the

108

fallen world could not continue to exist. They are indeed attempts of the creature, forerunners, but still the Messianic power itself is in them. "Messiah son of Joseph appears from generation to generation." That is the suffering Messiah who ever again endures mortal agony for the sake of God.

This Messianic mystery rests upon the hiddenness; not upon a secret attitude, but upon a genuine, factual hiddenness reaching into the innermost existence. The men through whom it passes are those of whom the nameless prophet speaks when he says, in the first person, that God sharpens them to a polished arrow and then conceals them in His quiver. Their hiddenness belongs to the essence of their work of suffering. Each of them can be the fulfilling one; none of them in his self-knowledge may be anything other than a servant of the Lord. With the tearing apart of the hiddenness not only would the work itself be suspended, but a counter-work would set in. Messianic self-disclosure is the bursting of Messiahship.

In order really to understand the relation of Judaism to the appearance of Jesus, one must descend into the depths of this faith, which is not condensed in any creed but can be shown from the testimonies. Whatever the appearance of Jesus means for the Gentile world (and its significance for the Gentile world remains for me the true seriousness of Western history), seen from the standpoint of Judaism he is the first in the series of men who, stepping out of the hiddenness of the servant of the Lord, the real "Messianic mystery," acknowledged their Messiahship in their souls

and in their words.* That this first one in the series
was incomparably the purest, the most legitimate, the
most endowed with real Messianic power—as I experience ever again when those personal words that ring
true to me merge for me into a unity whose speaker
becomes visible to me—alters nothing in the fact of this
firstness; indeed it undoubtedly belongs just to it, to
the fearfully penetrating reality that has characterized
the whole automessianic series.

To it undoubtedly also belongs the fact that the last
in this series—that Sabbatai Zvi who died in the same
year as Spinoza—sank into the deepest problematic,
slid over from an honest self-assurance into a pre-
tended one, and ended in apostasy. And it was not a
small band that clung to him, like the followers of the
earlier men in the series. Rather Jewry itself adhered to
him and accepted his statements as legitimate proclamations, statements which they once would have found
intolerable and would have taken as evidence against
any divine summons. It was, to be sure, a Jewry dis-
traught in an abyss of suffering, but it was still the
bearer of a real crisis: the self-dissolution of automes-
sianism. Always before, the people had resisted the
proclamations of the *"meshihim"* and its own thirst for
redemption. Now that it gave up its resistance this one

* This does not mean that Martin Buber thinks that Jesus himself necessarily saw himself as the Messiah, though he did
stand under the shadow of the Deutero-Isaianic servant of the
Lord. For Buber's full discussion of this difficult problem see
his *Two Types of Faith* (1951), Chapter X. See also below,
Supplement, "Christ, Hasidism, Gnosis," Section 2, for a fuller
treatment of this problem.—Ed.

time, the catastrophe prepared the end not merely of this one event, but of the whole form of the event: the meeting of a man who had taken the fateful step from the hiddenness of the servants of the Lord to Messianic self-consciousness, with a group who took it upon themselves to begin the kingdom of God.

In order to understand what is at stake here, it is necessary to recognize that it is not a question of what appears self-evident to our age, of the concurrence of two self-deceptions, one of a person and one of a group. It is a question of two real transgressions of a real boundary, a boundary on which man can move only with the anxious responsibility of the trembling needle of a magnet. The occurrences of the automessianic epoch of the Jewish faith in redemption (to which those of baptism in its varied forms correspond on the Christian side) were a mishap, but a mishap that befell the reality between man and God.

The Hasidic message of redemption stands in opposition to the Messianic self-differentiation of one man from other men, of one time from other times, of one act from other actions. All mankind is accorded the co-working power, all time is directly redemptive, all action for the sake of God may be Messianic action. But only unpremeditated action can be action for the sake of God. The self-differentiation, the reflexion of man to a Messianic superiority of this person, of this hour, of this action, destroys the unpremeditated quality of the act. Turning the whole of his life in the world to God and then allowing it to open and unfold in all its

111

moments until the last—that is man's work toward re-demption.

We live in an unredeemed world. But out of each human life that is unarbitrary and bound to the world, a seed of redemption falls into the world, and the harvest is God's.

# CHAPTER IV

# SPIRIT AND
# BODY OF THE
# HASIDIC MOVEMENT

# 1 SPIRIT

Movements that strive for a renewal of society mean by that for the most part that the axe should be laid to the root of the existing order; they set in contrast to what has come into being a fundamentally different product of willed thought. Not so the religious movements that proceed from a renewal of the soul. However much the principle that is advocated by a genuine religious movement may be diametrically opposed to the prevailing religious status of the environment, the movement experiences and expresses this opposition not as an opposition to the essential original content of the tradition; it feels and explains itself rather as summoned to purify this original content of its present distortions, to restore it, to "bring it back." But from this same starting-point the religious movements can progress very differently in their relation to the prevailing faith. On the one hand, the old-new principle may set its own message in bodily opposition to and as the original state of the late stage of the tradi-

114

tion. It presents its message, therefore, as the obscured original truth, now rescued and brought to light, represented by the central man "come" to restore it, and actually identical with him. Then the complete transformation and separation soon takes place. Such movements may be designated as founding ones. On the other hand, the principle may simply return to an older stage of the tradition, to the "pure word" that it has to liberate and whose distortion it combats. Then a partial separation takes place so that the mythical-dogmatic and magical-cultic fundamentals remain for the most part untouched, and, despite the organizational separation, the spiritual unity essentially continues. These movements are called reforming ones.

There is, however, a third possibility. The principle may accept the tradition in its present state with undiminished value; its teachings and precepts may be recognized in their full present extension without examining their historical credentials and without comparing them with an original form; but the principle creates a new *illumination* of the teachings and precepts, it makes it possible for it to win in this light a new soul, a new meaning, it renews their vitality without changing them in their substance. Here no separation takes place although here too the battle between the old and the new must break out and can take on the most violent forms: the new community remains within the hereditary one and seeks to penetrate it from within —a measuring of two forces against each other, the moving force and the conserving force, a measuring that is soon carried over to the ground of the new community itself and continues among its members, indeed within the heart of each individual. The conditions of the battle naturally become ever more favorable for the force of inertia. Among the movements of this type is the Hasidic which, beginning in Podolia and Wolhynia around the middle of the eighteenth century, by the turn of the century had taken possession of the Jewry of the whole Polish kingdom as well as important parts of North East Hungary and the Moldau and by the middle of the nineteenth century had developed into a structure benumbed in spirit but mighty in numbers that continues in existence to this day.

Genuine religious movements do not want to offer man the solution of the world mystery, but to equip him to live from the strength of the mystery; they do not wish to instruct him about the nature of God, but to show him the path on which he can meet God. But among them it is the third type of which I spoke that is most especially concerned not with a universally valid knowledge of what is and what ought to be but only about the here and now of the human person, the eternally new shoot of the eternal truth. Just for this reason, this movement can take over unchanged a system of general dogmas and precepts from the contemporary stage of the tradition; its own contribution cannot be codified, it is not the material of a lasting knowledge or obligation, only light for the seeing eye, strength for the working hand, appearing ever anew. This announces itself especially clearly in Hasidism. Of highest importance to it is not what has been from of old but what again and again happens; and, again,

116

not what befalls a man but what he does; and not the extraordinary that he does but the ordinary; and more still than what he does, how he does it. Among all the movements of this type probably none has proclaimed as clearly as Hasidism the infinite ethos of the moment.

Hasidism took over and united two traditions without adding anything essentially different to them other than a new light and a new strength: a tradition of religious law—next to the Vedic sacrificial teaching the most gigantic structure of spiritual commands—the ritual formation of Judaism; and a tradition of religious knowledge—inferior to gnosis in the power of its images, superior to it in systematization—the Kabbala.

These two streams of tradition were, of course, individually united in each Kabbalist, but their real fusion into one reality of life and community first took place in Hasidism.

The fusion took place through the old-new *principle* that it represented: the principle of the responsibility of man for God's fate in the world. Responsibility, not in a conditioned, moral, but in an unconditioned, transcendent sense, the mysterious, inscrutable value of human action, the influence of the acting man on the destiny of the universe, even on its guiding forces—that is an ancient idea in Judaism. "The righteous increase the might of the upper dominion." There is a causality of the deed that is withdrawn from our experience and only accessible to our intuitive gleanings.

This idea was elaborated in the development of the Kabbala to the central and sustaining role in which it

117

came forward in Hasidism: through the Kabbalistic concept of God's fate in the world.

Mythically living in the consequences of Iranian religiousness, conceptually outlined in many kinds of gnosis, the conception appears to us of the divine soul imprisoned in the material world, from which it must be redeemed. The splendor of light radiating from God that has sunk into the darkness, the Sophia that has fallen under the dominion of the lower powers that rule the world, the "Mother" who must walk through all the sufferings of the world of things—always it is a being mediating between primal good and primal evil whose fate is told: an abandoned being and yet a divine being, separated from its origins and yet not separated; for division means time and the unification eternity. The Kabbala has taken over the conception of the exiled divine soul, but has reforged it in the fire of the Jewish idea of unity which excludes a primal duality. The fate of the Glory of God, the "Indwelling" (Shekina), now no longer befalls it from its opposite, not from the powers of matter alienated from or in enmity to God, but from the necessity of the primal will itself; it belongs to the meaning of the creation.

How is the world possible? That is the basic question of the Kabbala, as it was the basic question of all gnosis. How can the world be since God still is? Since God is infinite, how can anything exist outside Him? Since He is eternal, how can time endure? Since He is perfect, how can imperfection come into being? Since He is unconditioned, why the conditioned?

The Kabbala * answers: God contracted Himself to world because He, nondual and relationless unity, wanted to allow relation to emerge; because He wanted to be known, loved, wanted; because He wanted to allow to arise from His primally one Being, in which thinking and thought are one, the otherness that strives to unity. So there radiated from Him the spheres: separation, creation, formation, making, the world of ideas, the forces, the forms, the material, the kingdom of genius, of spirit, of soul, of life; so there was established in them the All, whose "place" God is and whose center He is. The meaning of emanation, according to a Hasidic saying, is "not as the creatures suppose that the upper worlds should be above the lower ones, but the world of making is this one that appears to our material eye; however, if you fathom it deeper and disclose its materiality, then just this is the world of formation, and if you disclose it further, then it is the world of creation, and if you fathom its being still deeper, so it is the world of separation, and so until the Unlimited, blessed be He." The space-time world of the senses is only the outermost cover of God. There is no evil in itself; the imperfect is only cover and clasp of a more perfect.

By this is not meant that all world being is, in fact, mere appearance, but that it is a system of ever thicker coverings. And yet it is just this system in which God's fate fulfills itself. God has not, Himself fateless, made a world that experiences a fate: He Himself, as far as

* I do not consider here the development and declension of the Kabbalistic view, but only its basic content which was decisive for Hasidism.

He has sent it forth out of Himself, has clad Himself in it, dwells in it, He Himself in His Shekina has His fate in the world.

But why was the primal will not satisfied by the pure spheres of separation, the world of ideas, where He who willed to be known could be known face to face? Why must the act bring forth beyond itself ever "lower," more distant, shell-enclosed spheres, down to this obdurate, troubled, burdened world in which we creatures, we things live? Why could we not have remained ethereal genius, why had we one after the other to be soiled and permeated with fiery spirit, watery soul, earthly corporeal life?

To all such questions the Kabbala answers only: God contracted Himself to world. And it is answered. God wanted to be known, loved, wanted, that is: God willed a freely existing, in freedom knowing, in freedom loving, in freedom willing otherness; *he set it free.* This means the concept of *tsimtsum,* contradiction.* But while this power, taken away from eternal being, was accorded its freedom, the limitation of its freedom was set by nothing other than its own consequences; it flooded forth beyond its God-near purity. Becoming

---

* Gershom G. Scholem writes of *tsimtsum* that it is "one of the most amazing and far-reaching conceptions ever put forward in the whole history of Kabbalism. *Tsimtsum* originally means 'concentration' or 'contraction,' but if used in Kabbalistic parlance it is best translated by 'withdrawal' or 'retreat.' To the Kabbalist of Luria's school *Tsimtsum* does not mean the concentration of God *at* a point, but his retreat *away* from a point. . . . It means briefly that the existence of the universe is made possible by a process of shrinkage in God." *Major Trends in Jewish Mysticism,* Rev. ed. (New York: Schocken Books, 1946), p. 260 f.—Ed.

broke forth out of being, what the Kabbala calls "the mystery of the Breaking of the Vessels" took place. Sphere extended itself out of sphere, world climbed away over world, shell joined itself to shell, unto the limit of the transformations. Here, in the realm of matter that is extended in space, that endures in time, on the rim of what has become, in the uttermost border-land of sense things, God's wave breaks. The wave that breaks here is God's. As the light from the highest plunged into the lower spheres and shattered them, light-sparks from the primordial being in the immediate presence of God—the genius-natured Adam Kadmon—have fallen into the imprisonment of the things. God's Shekina descends from sphere to sphere, wanders from world to world, banishes itself in shell after shell until it reaches its furthest exile: us. In our world God's fate is fulfilled.

But our world is in truth the world of man.

In ancient Indian religion we encounter the myth of the "All-Sacrifice," the sacrifice of the primordial man out of whose parts the world was created. The conception of the primordial being, human in nature, that must perish or must abase himself in order that the separation of the worlds may take place, returns in Near-Eastern mystery rites and cultic hymns, cosmogonies and apocalypses. The Kabbala posits the Adam Kadmon in the beginning of the world's becoming as the figure of God and the archetype of the Universe, God's light his substance, God's name his life, the still quiescent elements of the spheres his limbs, all the opposites joined in him as right and left. The coming asunder of his parts is the coming to be of the world, it is also a sacrifice. But at its end, at the rim of that which has become, the event of all the breaking and darkening of the primordial light, grown out of the exuberant growth of the spheres, all opposites in him fallen apart into male and female, there stands again man, the mixed work of the elements, this earthly, singled-out individual, named, metabolically changing, innumerably born and dying man. In him the otherness that is left to its freedom has worked itself out to its last consequences, in him it has concentrated, and he, the latest, the most burdened of creatures, has from among them all, received the full heritage of freedom. Here first, in this child of corruption and light has there arisen the rightful subject of the act in which God wills to be known, loved, willed. Here is the movement to the end, only from here can "the Jordan flow upwards." Here the decision takes place.

In other teachings the God-soul, sent or released by heaven to earth, could be called home or freed to return home by heaven; creation and redemption take place in the same direction, from "above" to "below." But this is not so in a teaching which, like the Jewish, is so wholly based upon the double-directional relation of the human I and the divine Thou, on the reality of reciprocity, on the *meeting*. Here man, this miserable man is, by the very meaning of his creation, the helper of God. For his sake, for the sake of the "chooser," for the sake of him who can choose God, the world was created. Its shells are there in order that he may penetrate through them into the kernel. The spheres have

122

withdrawn from one another in order that he may bring them nearer to one another. The creature waits for him. God waits for him. From him, from "below" the impulse toward redemption must proceed. Grace is God's *answer.*

None of the upper, inner worlds, only this lowest and most external world is capable of providing the thrust to transformation in the *Olam Ha-Tikkun,* the world of completion, in which "the figure of the Shekina steps out of the hiddenness." For God has contracted Himself to world, He has set it free; now fate rests on its freedom. That is the mystery of man.

In the history of man the history of the world repeats itself. That which has become free overreaches itself. The "Fall into Sin" corresponds to the "Breaking of the Vessels." Both are signs of the necessary way. Within the cosmic exile of the Shekina stands the earthly exile, into which it is driven through the denial of man, going with him out of Paradise into wandering. And once again the history of the world repeats itself in that of Israel: its falling away is followed time after time—not as punishment but as consequence—by the exile in which the Shekina accompanies it, until the ultimate exile, where from now on, in the deepest abasement, "all depends on the turning." This joining of a cosmic conception with a historical one, accomplished by the Kabbala on the basis of ancient Jewish traditions, certainly contributed to making the concept of the system of emanations more direct and emotional; but at the same time the meaning and task of man was narrowed. All eschatology, indeed, is forever in danger,

123

through the confusion of absolute with historical categories, of sacrificing what is above time to the temporal, above all in an epoch where the eschatological vision is replaced by abstract construction. The finitizing of the end means the finitizing of the means: if the inwardness of Messianism, of the turning and transformation of the world, is forgotten, then there easily arises a theurgical praxis which wants to bring about redemption through formal procedures. This praxis exceeds itself in those powerful exaggerations of asceticism, an asceticism that strains after the void, which characterized the pre-Hasidic phase of the Kabbala and whose aftereffects entered into Hasidism, but mastered by its anti-ascetic tendency. But for the most part the great cosmogonic vision of the primordial man who embraced the spheres stands in contrast to a small scheme of redemption.

What Hasidism strives for as regards the Kabbala is the deschematization of the mystery. The old-new principle that it represented is, restored in purified form, that of the cosmic-metacosmic power and responsibility of man. "All worlds depend on his works, all gaze at and long for the teaching and the good deeds of man." This principle, which, by virtue of the pure intensity of Hasidism became a religious *meeting*, is no new element of teaching, as in general Hasidism included no new element of teaching; only here it has become, through suppression (not extirpation) of the violences, formal beliefs and mystosophies that manifoldly clung to it, a center of a life form and of a community. The eschatological impulse did not perish, the longing for the Messianic redemption found at times an even more personal expression in conjuring words and storming undertakings. But the work for the sake of the end subordinated itself to the continual working on the inner worlds through the hallowing of all action. In the stillness there ripened presentiments of a timeless salvation that the moment disclosed; no longer a set action but the dedication of all action became decisive. And as the mystery of present fulfillment joined the preparation of coming things, strengthening and illuminating it, winged joy lifted itself above asceticism as a butterfly above a cast-off cocoon.

Hasidism wants to "reveal God in this low, undermost world, in all things and at the same time in man that in him there be no limb and no movement in which God's strength might not be hidden, and none with which he could not accomplish unification." To the question of what service should come first, the Baal-Shem answered: "For the spiritual man this is the first: love without mortification; for the others this is the first: to learn to see that in all corporality is a holy life and that man can lead everything back to this its root and can hallow it."

One does not need to fast since whoever eats in dedication liberates the fallen sparks that are held captive in the food and that lend it fragrance and taste; even Haman was affected by the holiness of the meal when he was Esther's guest, and it is said of Abraham that he stood "above" the angels to whom he provided hospitality: because he knew the dedication of eating that was unknown to them. One does not need to forego

marital love since—as the Talmud already teaches—
where a man and a woman are together in holy unity,
the Shekina rests over them. After the death of his wife
the Baal-Shem would not let himself be comforted and
said: "I had hoped to journey to heaven in a thunder-
storm like Elijah, but now it has been taken from me,
for I am now only half of a body." One shall not mortify
himself; "he who does harm to his body, does harm to
his soul." The ascetic ecstasy is "from the other side,"
not of a divine, but of a demonic nature. One shall not
murder the "evil urge," the passion in oneself, but
serve God *with it;* it is the force that shall receive direction from man ("You have made the urge evil," God
already says to man in the Midrash). The "alien
thoughts," the lusts that come to man are pure ideas
that are corrupted in the "Breaking of the Vessels" and
now desire to be raised again by man. "Even the no-
blest bitterness touches on melancholy, but even the
most common joy grows out of holiness." One cannot
reach the kernel of the fruit except through the shell.
A zaddik cited the word of a Talmudic sage: "The
roads to the firmament are as illumined for me as the
roads of the city of Nehardea" and turned it around:
The streets of the city should be as light to one as the
paths of heaven; for "one cannot come to God except
through nature."

"Enoch was a cobbler. With every stitch of his awl
that sewed the upper leather and the sole together, he
joined God and His Shekina."

This wonderful contribution to the legend of the
patriarch who enjoyed companionship with God, was

taken away from earth and underwent transformation
into the demiurgic powerful Metatron, the fire-bodied
"Prince of the Countenance," was readily varied in the
Hasidic teaching. For in his earthly image he expresses
what was essential to it: that man influences eternity,
and he does this not through special works, but through
the intention behind all of his work. It is the teaching
of the hallowing of the everyday. It is of no value to
attain to a new type of action that is sacral or mystical
according to its material; what matters is that one does
the allotted tasks, the ordinary and obvious ones, in
their truth and in their meaning, and that means in
the truth and the meaning of all action.

Even one's works are shells; he who performs them
with the right dedication, embraces in kernel the
boundless.

On the basis of this view it is understandable why
Hasidism had no incentive to break loose any stick
from the structure of the traditional Law, for according
to the Hasidic teaching there could not exist anything
that was not to be fulfilled with intention or whose
intention could not be discovered. But it is also understandable how just thereby the conserving force secretly remained superior to the moving and renewing
one and finally conquered it within Hasidism itself.

Apart from this, no teaching finds it so difficult to
preserve its strength as one which places the meaning
of life in the working reality of the here and now and
does not tolerate man's fleeing before the taxing infinity of the moment into a uniform system of Is and
Ought; the inertia soon proves itself the stronger and

coerces the teaching. But in the short time of its purity the Hasidic teaching produced an immortal fullness of genuine life that did not withold itself.

# II  BODY

A teaching that places the unspecifiable "How" of an act high above the codifiable "What" is not able to hand down what is peculiar to it through writing; it is communicated ever again through life, by the leader to the community, but preferably from teacher to disciple. Not as though the teaching were divided into a part accessible to all and an esoteric realm; it would contradict its meaning, the work for man, if it concealed a secret drawer with hieratic inscription. Rather the mystery that is handed down is just that which is also proclaimed by the enduring word, only, true to its nature as a "How" it is only pointed to by the word, but in its substantial truth it can only be presented through authentication.

Hence a "hidden zaddik" said of the rabbis who "say Torah," that is, interpret the word of the Scriptures, "What is it that the Torah says? Man shall heed that all his conduct should be a Torah and himself a Torah." And another time it says: "The wise man shall aspire that he himself be a perfected teaching and all his deeds bodies of instruction; or, where this is not granted him, that he be a transmission and exposition of the teaching and that the teaching should spread through each of his movements." A sacramental expression of this basic insight appears when the zaddik of Apt lifts up the girdle, fallen to the ground, of the seventeen-year-old Rabbi Israel, later the Rishiner, girds it round him and says that in so doing he performs the holy action of Gelila: the unfolding of the Torah-scroll.

The men in whom "being a Torah" fulfills itself are called zaddikim, "the righteous," the legitimate ones. They bear the Hasidic teaching, not only as its apostles, but as its working reality. They are the teaching.

In order to grasp the special significance of the zaddik in contrast, for example, to the Russian *staretz*, as Dostoevsky has presented him with the transfiguring fidelity of the great poet, one must call to mind the fundamental difference between Judaism's conception of history and that of Christianity (or that of another savior religion, for example, Buddhism). What is decisive is not the conception of redemption itself: this already lived in prophetic Messianism and was developed by post-exilic Judaism to the core of its world view. But to the savior religions redemption is a fact—one by its nature transcending history, nonetheless localized in it; to Judaism it is a pure prospect. For Christianity the historical age ("the present aeon") has a caesura, an absolute center in which, as it were, it erupts, until the ground is split open, and just thereby it gains its henceforth imperturbable base. For Judaism history, without any such central mooring point and left entirely to its never-ceasing flow, must strive for "the end." Thus in Christianity (as in Buddhism) the decisive has taken place and can from now on only be "imitated," renewed only in union, only be repeated. In Judaism the decisive takes place at all times, that is: it takes place here and now. Before the flowering fullness of fate of the here and now the horizon of "the last things" visibly pales: the kingdom of God seems to be projected in time onto the horizon of the absolute future where heaven and earth meet; the timeless present reveals itself ever again in the moment where, out of the essential act of the true man, the unification of God and His Shekina takes place. It was, to be sure, a Christian, western seer who confronted his church with the statement: "The noble man is that only-begotten Son of God whom the Father eternally begets." * But in none of the Christian heretical groups that might wish to take that view seriously could it thrive into unequivocal life. In Hasidism there arose— as a reality that was weak, condemned to decay from the beginning, yet nonetheless imperishable—the Jewish companion saying in which in place of the "begetting," the unbroken grace streaming down, stands the meeting of divine activity with the human, in which, however, the word "eternally" resounds with equal strength.

The zaddik is not a priest or a man who renews in himself an already-accomplished work of salvation or transmits it to his generation, but the man who is more concentratedly devoted than other men to the task of salvation that is for all men and all ages, the man whose

* One of the propositions of Meister Eckhart condemned by the Pope in 1329.

forces, purified and united, are directed toward the one duty. He is, according to the conception of him, the man in whom transcendental responsibility has grown from an event of consciousness into organic existence. He is the true human being, the rightful subject of the act in which God wants to be known, loved, wanted. In him the "lower," earthly man realizes his archetype, the cosmic primordial man who embraces the spheres. He is the turning of the great flood, in him the world returns to its origin. He is "no slave of time, but above it." He bears the lower blessing upward and the upward below; he draws down the Holy Spirit over men. The being of the zaddik works in the higher realms. He must "boil the great pots" with his fire—so one zaddik once spoke of another in a hearty and perceptive jesting word. In him the world renews itself, he is its "foundation" (so the word concerning the "righteous" in Proverbs 10:25 is interpreted). "The zaddik is the foundation because with his works he incessantly awakens the outpouring of the fullness over the world. And if it is perfected in him that all his action takes place only for the sake of uniting the Shekina with God, then there comes over his soul a stream of grace from the holy fullness that pours forth from out of the light of God's unity, and he is become like a new creature and like a little child that was just born. This is that which is written: 'And unto Shem was also born he . . .' * For whoever values God alone in all his work, he begets himself in the renewal of the light of his soul."

* Interpretive translation of Genesis 10:21.

A true man is more important than an angel because the latter is "one who stands," but he is "one who walks"; he advances, penetrates, ascends. Constant renewal is the characteristic life principle of the zaddik. In him creation's event of becoming concentrates itself into creative meaning, the genuine meaning, wholly free from arbitrariness and self-seeking, which is nothing other than just the turning of the creation to the Creator. The zaddik incessantly beholds directly the bodily renewal of all and "is moved at each moment by the renewal of the creature"; his being answers with the renewal of the spirit. And as the bodily renewal in nature is always accompanied by a submersion, a dissolution, a sleep of the elements, so there is no true spiritual becoming without a ceasing to become. "For the zaddikim," says Rabbi Sussya, "who in their service go ever again from holiness to holiness and from world to world, must, to begin with, cast their life from them in order to receive a new spirit, that a new illumination may sweep over them ever again; and this is the mystery of sleep." The symbolic act that corresponds to this event of deep inwardness is the immersion bath. Primeval symbol of rebirth (which is only genuine when it includes death and resurrection), taken up into Kabbalistic praxis out of old traditions, especially those of the Essenes and the "morning-baptists," it is practiced by the zaddikim with a high and joyous passion that has nothing of the ascetic in it. It is told of many how during the severest frost of winter they broke the ice of the stream in order to immerse themselves in flowing water; and the meaning of this fervor is revealed in the statement of a Hasid that one could replace the immersion bath by a spiritual act, that of the "stripping away of bodiliness." What is here expressed in the action is preparation and readiness to enter into the "condition of the nothing," in which alone the divine renewal can take place.

In this ever-new exercise of the "receiving power" of the zaddik, the ever-new dedication of his acting power takes place. Armed with rejuvenated strength, he goes ever again to his work—to his daily work: to the thousandfold work of "unification," the *yihud.*

*Yihud* means, first of all, both the unity of God and the confession of it that is to the Jew not only the central sun of his religion, but of his life system in general. Even so, however, this confession already represents, not a passive acknowledgment, but an act. It is in no way the statement of a subject about an object; it is not "subjective" at all, but a subjective-objective event, an event of meeting, it is the dynamic form of the divine unity itself. This active character of *yihud* grows in the Kabbala, matures in Hasidism. Man *works on* the unity of God, that is: through him takes place the unity of becoming, the divine unity of creation. By its nature, to be sure, *yihud* can always mean only unification of what has been separated. It is a unification, however, which overarches the enduring differences and finds its cosmic counterpart: the unity without multiplicity which dwells in the unification of multiplicity.

It is of fundamental importance to contrast the characteristic conception of *yihud* with *magic* action. The

133

magic act means the influence of a subject on an object, of a man versed in magic on a "power"—a divine or demonic, personal or impersonal power, appearing in the world of things or concealed behind it. Thus it is a constitutive duality of elements of which the one, the human, is, by its fundamental nature, the weaker. But by virtue of this man's magic ability, it becomes the stronger, the compelling. It compels the other, the divine or the demonic, into human service, into human intention, into human work. The man from whom the act proceeds is also its goal and end; the magic act is an isolated, circular causal process which turns back in on itself. *Yihud* signifies not the influence of a subject upon an object, but the working out of the objective in a subjectivity and through it, of existing being in and through what is becoming; a true, serious, and complete working out, indeed, so that what is becoming is not a tool that is moved but a self-mover that is freed, free, acting out of freedom; world history is not God's game, but God's fate. *Yihud* means the ever-new joining of the spheres striving to be apart, the ever-new marriage of the "majesty" with the "Kingdom"—through man; the divine element living in man moves from him to God's service, to God's intention, to God's work; God, in whose name and by whose command of creation the free *yihud* takes place, is his goal and end, he himself turning not in himself but to God, not isolated, but swallowed in the world process, no circle but the swinging back of the divine strength that was sent forth.

This distinction explains why magic must include a

qualitative special action that is supposed to produce the special effect: gestures and speeches of a particular nature alien to other men and other moments. *Yihud,* in contrast, means no special formula or procedure but nothing other than the ordinary life of man, only concentrated and directed to the goal of unification. Many Kabbalistic traditions of the secret of the letters (of the alphabet), the turning round and joining of the names of God, were taken up and practiced by Hasidism, it is true, in its system of *kavanot,* or intentions; but this magic ingredient never touched the center of Hasidic teaching. In this center stand no secret formulae but the dedication of everything: no deed is condemned by its nature to remain "profane," each becomes service and influence on the divine if it is directed toward the unification, that means revealed in its inner dedication. The life of the zaddik is borne by this all-pervading might of *yihud.*

It is told of the zaddik of Berditshev how in his youth, while a guest of his friend the Nikolsburger Rabbi, he aroused general indignation because, wrapped in the prayer shawl and with the double phylacteries on his forehead, he went into the kitchen and inquired about the preparation of the food, and because later in the prayer house he entered into a conversation with the most worldly man about all kinds of apparently frivolous things. Desecration of the holy garments, desecration of the holy place and the holy hour were laid to his charge; but the Master spoke: "What I can only do three hours in the day, he can do the whole day: to preserve his spirit collected so that even with talk that passes as idle he can bring about exalted unifications." Hallowing of the worldly is the central motive of the zaddik. His meal is a sacrifice, his table an altar. All his movements lead to salvation. It is told of one that in his youth he went day after day into the villages and transacted business with the peasants; and always, when he had returned home and said the afternoon prayer he felt all his limbs permeated by a blessed fire. He asked his older brother, who was also his teacher, what this was, for he feared that it might come to him from evil and that his service was false. The brother answered: "When you go over the field in a holy state of mind, all the sparks of souls that are in stones, plants and animals cling to you and purify themselves in you to a holy fire."

This consecration of the everyday is above all magic. When in the days of Rabbi Pinhas of Koretz the whole prayer book of Rabbi Isaac Luria, the master of the theurgic Kabbala, the prayer book composed of letter-kavanot, was published, the disciples of the zaddik requested his permission to pray out of it; but after some time they came to him again and complained that since they had prayed out of the book, they had suffered a great loss of the feeling of vital life in their prayers. Rabbi Pinhas answered them: "You have put all your strength and all your striving for the goal of your thoughts into the *kavanot* of the holy names and the intertwined letters and have fallen away from what is essential: to make the heart whole and to unite it to God—therefore you have lost the life and feeling of

136

holiness." All formulas and arts are patchwork; the
true unification rises beyond them. "He who in his
prayer," says the Baal-Shem, "employs all the *kavanot*
that he knows, effects only just what he knows. But he
who speaks the word with great binding to God, for
him all *kavana* enters of itself into each word." What
matters is not what can be learned, what matters is
giving oneself to the unknown.

A zaddik said: "Note well, that the word Kabbala
stems from *kabbel,* to receive, and the word *kavana*
from *kaven,* to direct outward. For the ultimate meaning of all the wisdom of the Kabbala is to take upon
oneself the yoke of God's kingdom, and the ultimate
meaning of all the art of *kavana* is to direct one's heart
to God. When one says: 'God is mine, and I am His'—
how is it that his soul does not leave his body?" As
soon as he had said this, he fell into a deep swoon from
which he was awakened only with great difficulty.

It becomes clear here that *yihud* means a risk, *the*
risk. The unification of God shall take place in the
world, man shall work on God's unification out of his
own unification—the human, earthly salvation, earthly
understanding, earthly life must be risked for the
divine. This is manifested most powerfully in prayer.
It is told of one zaddik that every day before he went
to pray, he ordered his household as if he were going
to die. Another taught his disciples how they should
pray: "He who speaks the word 'Lord' and at the same
time has in mind speaking the word, 'of the world,'
this is no speaking. Rather during the time when he
says 'Lord,' he should in his mind offer himself wholly

137

to the Lord so that his soul might perish in the Lord and he no longer be able to utter the word 'world' and it would be enough for him that he could say 'Lord.' This is the essence of prayer." The Baal-Shem-Tov compared the ecstatic movements of the Hasid, who prayed with his whole body, to the movements of a drowning man.

It was also told of some zaddikim, as before of certain Talmudic masters, how the ecstasy of prayer powerfully governed their bodies and carried them away to movements far beyond those of the ordinary human world. About many in such moments there was a remoteness as about a holy madman. But all this is only an event of the threshold and not the entrance, it is the struggling risk and not the fulfillment. Rabbi Yehuda Loeb tells how once during the Feast of Booths he witnessed in the tabernacle before the benediction the movements of the great zaddik of Lublin who seemed driven as if by a secret dread. All the people stared fixedly at him and themselves fell into a trembling fear, but Rabbi Yehuda Loeb remained seated and waited until the benediction; then he stood up, looked at the now motionless, exalted master and heard the divine blessing. Thus Moses had once paid no attention to the thunder claps and the smoking mountain that the trembling people surrounded and had drawn near the motionless cloud.

The less premeditated the prayer is, the more immediately it breaks forth out of the natural depths of man, out of the cosmic spontaneity of him who bears the image of the sphere-embracing primordial man, so

much the more real it is. It is told of a disciple of a
disciple of the Lubliner zaddik, Rabbi Mendel of
Kotzk, probably the last great figure of Hasidism,
that he prayed without effort and strain, as one con-
verses with a comrade, and yet after the prayer was
transformed as though he came from another world,
and scarcely recognized his own family; "for the nature
of his talk proceeds from the root of the soul unintentionally; as one whose soul is occupied with a very important subject at times unintentionally allows words to
issue from his mouth between him and himself, and he
himself does not notice his talk, and all this because it
proceeds from the root of his soul, and the whole soul is
wrapped in the speech which ascends in perfect unity."
Here, in genuine prayer, there appears most clearly the
essential meaning of *yihud*, that it is no "subjective"
happening, but the dynamic form of the divine unity itself. "The people imagine," says Rabbi Pinhas of Koretz,
"that they pray before God. But this is not so. For
prayer itself is the essence of divinity."

Of such kind is the lonely service of the zaddik. But
he is not a true zaddik who remains satisfied with this.
Man's bond with God authenticates and fulfills itself in
the human world.

Rabbi Hayim of Zans was once bothered after the
*minha* prayer by an importunate man with a request.
As the man would not desist, the zaddik addressed him
angrily. Questioned by a friend who was present as
to the cause of his wrath, he answered, that he who
prays the *minha* stands over against the world of
primordial sundering; how should he not become angry

when he comes from it and now is fallen upon by the petty cares of petty people? To this the other said: "After the Bible has told of the first proclamation of God to Moses on Mount Sinai, it says, 'Moses descended from the mountain to the people.' Rashi comments on this as follows: 'This teaches us that Moses turned from the mountain not toward his own affairs but to the people.' How is that to be understood? What sort of business did Moses have in the wilderness that he renounced in order to go to the people? But it is to be understood thus: When Moses descended from the mountain, he still cleaved to the upper worlds and accomplished in it his high work of penetrating the sphere of justice with the element of mercy. That was Moses's business. And still, when he descended to the people, he desisted from his high work, disengaged himself from the upper worlds and turned himself to the people; he listened to all its small cares, stored up all the heaviness of heart of all Israel and then bore them upward in prayer." When Rabbi Hayim heard this, his spirit became serious and profound, he called back the man whom he had addressed angrily, in order to receive his request and almost the whole night through he received the complaints and requests of the assembled Hasidim.

"Above" and "below"—the decisive importance is ascribed to the "below." Here on the outermost margin of having become, the fate of the aeons is decided. The human world is the world of authentication. "Do not be bad before yourself," that is, do not imagine yourself unredeemable, it is written in *The Sayings of the*

140

*Fathers.* But Rabbi Baruch, the grandson of the Baal-Shem, interprets the saying otherwise: "Each man is called to bring something in the world to completion. Each one is needed by the world. But there are men who sit continually shut up in their chambers and learn and do not step out of the house to converse with the others; for this reason they are called bad. For if they would converse with the others, they would bring to completion something of what is allotted to them. This means: do not be bad 'before yourself'; what is meant is: do not be bad in that you stay before yourself and do not go to men; do not be bad through solitude."

The love of man is not the fulfillment of an otherworldly commandment; it is the work on the completion, it helps the shape of the Shekina to step forth out of the hiddenness, it works on the "wagon": on the cosmic bearer of liberated glory. Therefore it is written: "Love your fellow as one like yourself: *I am the Lord.*" The kingdom is founded on love.

Therefore Rabbi Raphael of Bershad, Rabbi Pinhas' favorite disciple, always used to warn against being "moderate" in one's dealings with one's fellowmen: Excess in love is necessary in order to make up for the lack in the world.

There are three circles in which the love of the zaddik is authenticated.

The first and broadest encompasses the many who come to the zaddik from a distance, partly—especially on the high holidays—to spend a few days near him, "in the shadow of his holiness," partly to ask help from him for their bodily and spiritual needs. In this pil-

grimage there is something of that faithful and trusting
spirit with which the Palestinians once went to the
Temple in Jerusalem three times a year in order
through sacrifice to free themselves from evil and join
themselves with the divine: "the zaddik takes the place
of the altar." To be sure, on the slips of paper they
hand in, mostly quite external lacks and wants are set
down. But the healing of these lacks at the same time
touches the inmost depths and stirs it to transforming
reflection. For the understanding of the general phenomenon that underlies this particular working of the
zaddik, a working whose factual nature cannot be con-
tested, the concepts "wonder" and "suggestion" con-
tribute very little. The first dissipates the irrationality
of the phenomenon, the second makes shallow its ability to be rationalized. To try to explain it as the working of the divine on the human offers a much too vague
perspective, as the influence of the "stronger" will on
the "weaker" a much too narrow one. One can best do
justice to its deeper dimension when one bears in mind
that the relation of a soul to its organic life depends on
the degree of its wholeness and unity. The more disso-
ciated the soul, the more it is at the mercy of its sick-
nesses and attacks, the more concentrated it is, the
more it is able to master them. It is not as if it conquered the body; rather through its unity it ever again
saves and protects the unity of the body. This power
rules suddenly and unmistakably where in a dispersed
soul in an elemental moment it accomplishes a crystallization and unification; there takes place rapidly
and visibly there what otherwise only grows in vege-

tative darkness, the "healing." Through nothing else can this process be effected so simply and directly as through the psychosynthetic appearance of a whole, united soul laying hold of the dispersed soul, agitating it on all sides, and demanding the event of crystallization. It does not "suggest"; it fashions in the fellow-soul by which it is called, a ground and center, and the more genuinely and fully, the more it is concerned that the appealing soul that calls it does not remain dependent on it: the helper establishes ground and center not in order that he might install his own image in the soul that is to be rebuilt, but in order that it might look through him, as through a glass, into being and now discover being in itself and let it be empowered as the core of living unity. Only the greatest of the zaddikim have performed this task adequately. They stand in the ranks of God's helpers.

The second, middle circle includes those who live in the neighborhood of the zaddik. This represents, in general, only a part of the Jewish community of that place, the rest consisting of the "opponents" (*Mitnagdim*) and the indifferent, whose official spiritual leader is the "rav." Inside the Jewish community, which is a "compulsory community," stands the Hasidic, a free, a "chosen community," with the zaddik, the "rebbe" at its head (yet several zaddikim have also exercised the functions of the rav in the Hasidic-dominated communities and have borne his title). This difference corresponds to that between the legitimation of the rav and that of the rebbe. The qualification of the rav is the demonstrated knowledge of the law in its Talmudic

roots and in the whole fullness of its rabbinical ramifi-
cations. The qualifications of the rebbe are the sponta-
neously acknowledged leadership of souls, the depth
of his "fear of God," that is, the dominant feeling of
the *presence* of God, and the fervor of his "heart service," that is, the shaping of his whole life to active
prayer.

This in no ways means, of course, that these qualities
were to be found only among the zaddikim and not
also among the traditional rabbis, just as little as it
means that many of the zaddikim did not possess a
comprehensive and independently developing knowledge of Halacha (the Law). The greatest of the opponents of Hasidism, Rabbi Elija of Vilna, was an
interpreter of the Book Zohar, the foundation of the
Kabbala, and the most important systematizer of Hasidism, Rabbi Shneur Zalman, was the author of a ritual
code of law; and if one juxtaposes the two life-histories
that tradition has handed down, it is not the second but
the first that has the mystical-legendary character. One
must guard against comprehending pragmatically instead of dialectically the antithesis that is inevitable in
the contemplation of the inner history; the movement
of the spirit takes place in contradiction, but it does
not embody itself in it. With this qualification, the
Hasidic community may be regarded as the social
representation of the principle of spontaneity, the
zaddik as the representative of autonomous leadership.
The strongest manifestation of both and of their unity
is the communal prayer; it is the regularly recurring
and yet ever-new symbolic act of the unification of

zaddik and community. The musty, overfull hall of the Beth-ha-Midrash,* where the poor wanderers slept at night and the sharp disputes over the Talmud resounded in early morning, now breathes the air of mystery. Even where the zaddik prays in a separate room, he is bound into one being with his community.

The third, narrowest circle is that of the disciples, of whom several are usually taken into the household community of the zaddik. This is the proper sphere of the transmission, the communication of the teaching from generation to generation.

Each of the three circles has its unity in the strength of the *reciprocal action.* Of the "journeying ones" Rabbi Pinhas said, "Often when one comes to me to ask advice, I hear how he himself speaks the answer." Of the community, especially those who pray, the Baal-Shem told the parable of the bird's nest that many people set themselves to fetch from the top of a very high tree, each standing on the shoulder of the other and he himself standing at the top; what if the time had been too long for only one of them! But the might of reciprocity is represented at its greatest in the third circle.

Some disciples of Rabbi Nahum of Tshernobil sat once in a distant city at "the farewell meal for the Queen" that unites the pious once again at the departure of the Sabbath, and they talked among themselves of the reckoning that the soul has to render in the innermost self-recollection of the self. Then they were overcome in their fear and humility so that it

* General house of prayer and study.

145

seemed to them as if their whole life were thrown away and wasted, and they said to one another that there would be no more hope for them if there were not this one consolation and assurance that they might join themselves to the great zaddik Rabbi Nahum. Then they arose with a common impulse and set out on the way to Tshernobil. At the same time Rabbi Nahum sat in his house and rendered the account of his soul. Then it also seemed to him in his fear and humility that his life was thrown away and wasted and all his assurance lay only in this one thing, that these God-impassioned men had joined themselves to him. He went to the door and looked across toward the dwelling-place of the disciples; and when he had stood there awhile, he saw them coming. "In that moment," added the grandson of the zaddik when he related the happening, "the circle was closed."

As the reciprocal value finds expression here, so in another story the reciprocal influence. Rabbi Susya once sat on his chair on one of the days of heart-searching between New Year's and the Day of Atonement, and the Hasidim stood around him from morning till evening. He had raised his eyes and heart to heaven and freed himself from all corporal bonds. Looking at him awakened in one of the disciples the impulse to the turning, and the tears rushed down his face; and as from a burning ember the neighboring coals begin to glow, so the flame of the turning came over one man after another. Then the zaddik looked around him and regarded them all. He raised his eyes again and spoke to God: "Truly, Lord of the world, it is the right time to turn back to you; but you know, indeed, that I have not the strength for atonement—so accept, my love and my shame as atonement!" It is this kind of influence that I have pointed to as that handing on of the mystery that is above words.

Ever again it says in the Hasidic writings that one should "learn from every limb of the zaddik." It is the spontaneity of his existence above all that exercises the purifying and renewing influence; the conscious expression, and above all, that of words, only accompanies it. Even in the word the essence of the unintentional is what is decisive.

"Make me an altar from the earth of the field," it says in the Scripture; "but if you make me an altar of stone, do not build it of hewn stone, for if you have swung your iron over it, then you have profaned it." The altar made out of earth, so the Rishiner expounded, that is what pleases God above all else, it is the altar made out of silence; but if you make an altar out of words, then do not shape them.

The zaddik shunned the "beautiful," the premeditated. A learned man who was a Sabbath guest at Rabbi Baruch's table, said to him: "Let us now hear words of teaching; you speak so beautifully!" "Before I speak beautifully," answered the grandson of the Baal-Shem, "may I become dumb!" and spoke no further.

At the holiest of the Sabbath meals, the "third meal," the zaddik usually speaks the teaching only sparingly and disconnectedly, ever again interrupted by silent meditation; a soft song, vibrating with mystery, sounds forth, an enraptured anthem follows. As often as the silence enters the darkening room, it brings a rustling of eternity with it.

The three circles in which the love of the zaddik is authenticated—the crowd, streaming to and from, of those seeking help, the community bound together in the connection of space and life, the strong ring of souls of the disciples—exhibit the forces out of which the vitality of the Hasidic movement was built up. Its spiritual structure was founded upon the handing on of the kernel of the teaching from teacher to disciple, but not as if something not accessible to everyone, was transmitted to him, but because in the atmosphere of the master, in the spontaneous working of his being, the inexpressible How descended swinging and creating. The very same teaching, only blended and less condensed, was communicated in the word of counsel and instruction, and was developed in the customs and brotherly life of the community. This absence of ranks in the sphere of its teaching, this anti-hierarchical position insured Hasidism its popular power. As it did not abolish from without the precedence of possession, but removed its value from within through uniting rich and poor as equal members, before God and the zaddik, of a community of reciprocal outer and inner help, a community of love; so it overcame, in its highest moments fully, the far stronger, in Judaism elementally strong, precedence of learning, the Talmudic but also the Kabbalistic. The "spiritual" man, the man who works with his brains, is by his nature no closer to the divine, indeed, so long as he has not gathered the multi-

148

plicity and ambiguity of his life into unity, so long as he has not subdued the violence of his pains to composure, he is farther from the divine than the simple man who, with the simple trust of the peasant, leaves his cause to heaven.

This combination of purity of teaching and popular character is made possible by the basic content of Hasidic teaching, the hallowing of everything worldly. There is no separation within the human world between the high and the low; to each the highest is open, each life has its access to reality, each nature its eternal right, from each thing a way leads to God, and each way that leads to God is *the* way.

# CHAPTER V

# SYMBOLIC AND
# SACRAMENTAL EXISTENCE

# I SYMBOLIC EXISTENCE
## IN THE WORLD OF PROPHECY

Human existence is not merely the space in which symbols and sacraments appear, and not merely the material with which they clothe themselves. The real existence of a human person can itself be symbol, itself be sacrament.

It does not belong to the nature of the symbol to float timelessly above the concrete actualities. Its ability to appear at any time always stems from the unforeseeable uniqueness of its appearance, its appearing for the first time. The symbol derives its enduring character from its transitoriness. Certainly, on the rim of the lived world we can acknowledge that everything transitory is "only" a simile *; but when we live in it, we learn that only the transitory can become simile. As image of unbroken meaning, as its own expression— in contrast to which all that we call speech is only

* "Alles Vergängliche ist nur ein Gleichnis," Goethe, *Faust* II, Act V.—Ed.

rough estimate—the symbol always serves in the first instance nothing else than our born, mortal body— everything else is only repetition, simplification, imitation. The spiritual with its timeless works is a closed circle; it does not point beyond itself; the time-imprisoned body alone can become transparent in its passing gestures. The covenant that the absolute forms with the concrete, beyond the general—the "idea"— ever again selects for itself a sign more fleeting than the rainbow of Noah's covenant: movement of a human figure, attitude or action. And this sign endures. It may, of course, lose in immediate validity, in "credibility," but it can also be renewed out of new human existence that fulfills anew. Every symbol is always in danger of changing from a real sign sent into life into a spiritual and unbinding image, every sacrament of changing from a bodily event between above and below into a flat experience on the "religious" plane. Only through the man who devotes himself is the strength of the origin saved for further present existence.

Plato distinguishes in the *Timaeus* (72B) between the *"manteis"* and the *"prophetai."* The "manteis" are the diviners, whom he understands as *"manentes,"* raving ones, enraptured by the god and "foretelling" in enigmatic sounds what they have received from him. The "prophetai" are the "proclaimers," who interpret the mysterious sound and translate it into human speech. Only the passive element in it recedes, but the essential relationship remains the same when

153

Pindar * assigns to the Muse the "foretelling," to the poet the "proclaiming": she inspires in him the primal sound, he shapes it in word and verse; but she herself does not express herself, but the god, her lord Apollo, by whom she, a superhuman Pythia, is possessed. And even he—so he confesses in Aeschylus †—serves as *mantis* and prophet combined to a higher, Zeus, who bestows upon him knowledge; he utters it, but him whom his speech lays hold of, Muse or Pythia, perceives no word, only mystery that is whispered forth, not expressed, until, at last, its hearer, the "prophetic" interpreter, proclaims it.

The *manteia*, the divination, is not yet "finished" speech to the Greeks. It breaks forth, uncomprehended and to the non-prophetic man incomprehensible, and is only grasped by the prophets and formed to *logos*. The prophet translates, but from a language that is no language to the ear of him who is not called. Where a man unites both offices, we must assume that he is actually first *mantis* and then prophet; in the place of the differentiation in the person comes a differentiation in the condition, a transformation in the person. The duality remains.

Not so with the Biblical *nabi*. It is not without significance, in the first place, that the concept is not here too used in a secular sense, as in the Greek where one can also call the expounder of a philosophy, yes even the herald in an athletic game, a prophet, as one who announces, publicly proclaims something. The *nabi*

* *Fragment* 150.
† *Eumenides,* v. 17 ff. (cf. 615 ff.).

only exists in the relation between deity and humanity, as the mediator of the speech, the "bearer of the word in the vertical plan," * and, in fact, not merely from above to below, the bringer of a divine message, but also from below to above: it is as "proclaimer" that Abraham shall "interpose himself as mediator" for the Philistine king (that is the basic meaning of the Hebrew term for "to pray"), it is as "proclaimer" that Miriam sings, that Deborah sings her thanksgiving song of victory. The *nabi's* task is to enable the spoken dialogue between deity and humanity to fulfill itself. God chooses for Himself this messenger "from in his mother's womb," in order that through him the admonishing and promising primal call may strike the ear of the hearer, but also in order that in him the cry from the heart of the creature may concentrate and through him be uplifted. Certainly, the divine intention does not aim at mediation, but at immediacy; but the mediator is the way to it—to the longed-for time when all God's people shall become proclaimers and bearers of the spirit (Numbers 11:29).

The Biblical concept of the *nabi* becomes clearest in one place (Exodus 7:1) where it is used as a simile: where two men are placed in just the relationship to each other of Elohim, the power of God. and the *nabi,* its proclaimer. "See," God says there to Moses, "I give you to Pharaoh as an Elohim, and Aaron, thy brother, shall be thy *nabi.*" The simile allows both, Elohim, the inspiring power, and the *nabi,* the expressing being, to

---

* Martin Buber, *Königtum Gottes,* 3rd Ed. (Heidelberg: Verlag Lambert Schneider, 1956), p. 136.

appear here unmistakably in their mutual over-against-
ness. How intimate this mutuality is meant to be is
expressed at an earlier stage of the narrative by a
parallel passage (4:16): "He therefore speaks for you
to the people, and so be it: he becomes a mouth for you
and you become an Elohim for him." To be the *nabi* of
an Elohim thus means to be his "mouth." His mouth,
not his mouthpiece: the *nabi* does not convey a finished speech that has already become audible; rather
he shapes to sound a secret, soundless speech, in the
human sense, pre-verbal, in the divine, primordially
verbal, as the mouth of a person shapes to sound the
secret, soundless speech of his innermost being. This
basic conception attains its full pathos when God
speaks of His relation to the *nabi* in this same image
and the Biblical distance between God and man is still
perserved through the fact that He says not "my
mouth," but "as my mouth." Jeremiah, in a critical hour,
implored God for vengeance on his persecutors (15:15).
He who answers him not only does not accede to the
request by which the prophet has become unfaithful
to his office: He gives him to understand (v. 19 f.) that
only when he finds the way back from the all-too-
human path on which he has strayed to the way of
God will He reinstate him and allow him to stand
"before His face": "If you bring forth the genuine,
freed of the base, you shall become as my mouth."

It is decisively important to observe that God does
not say here that he wants to use the human mouth as
His own: *the whole human person* shall be as a mouth
to him.

156

That the Greek prophet is not and cannot be. His mouth "speaks forth," not his person. But the mantis too is not it and cannot be it. His person, seized and possessed by the god, utters, but it does not speak forth. So long as one functions as mantis, he remains incomprehensible to him who receives his speech; as soon as he becomes his own prophet, he is still only the speaker of a word removed from him.

In the Biblical world of faith there are not two who stand over against God, one immediately and the other mediately, but one; just he whom the divine "storm of the spirit" inspires in order "to clothe itself with him" (Judges 6:34), is he who, not with his instruments of speech alone, but with his whole being and life, is speaker of the hidden voice, that "hovering silence" (1 Kings 19:12), that blows through him.

"Pythia and interpreting priestly poet were not here separated: the Israelite prophet was both in one person" (Max Weber). For the prophetic word of the Bible, in contrast to that of the Delphic oracle, means that the originating speech and the finished speech are Biblically identical, whereas in the Hellenic an ecstatic babbling must first be transmitted into ordered speech. The speech which breaks forth from the Biblical proclaimers is already coined into words, rhythmically joined, "objective." And yet it is not a word detachable from its speaker so that it is only "conveyed by the mouth": the whole personal spokenness belongs to it, the whole speaking human body, animated in itself and now inspired by the *ruach*, the pneuma, the whole

157

existence of this man belongs to it, the whole man is mouth.

Here there is no division between a passion of "*mainesthai,*" possessions and rapture, and an action of "*proeipein,*" the overpowering, formative speech. The form of the speech is here not "received," it is born in the primal urge to articulation—wherefore, for example, even all metrical schematization must ever again fail here in the hands of the scholars because the "ready-made" meter is every time overturned by the unique stream of prophecy. The man who is seized by the *ruach* and compelled to words does not stammer before he speaks; in the "grasp of the hand" he still speaks a rhythmically strict speech, yet one through which the cascading fullness of the moment has streamed.

The thesis of a "development" from the "primitive ecstatic" to the "word-prophet" is also misleading: in the Bible the ecstatic never appears except in conjunction with the word-prophet; we do, indeed, read of wild, "raving"—yet not unmusical—conduct, but not of unarticulated babbling or shouting; we come to know the voice of the *nabi* only as word, his word only as speech. In historical time, moreover, passion and action are not here divided, but one. What is in question is a single, all-embracing function, and the undivided person is needed in order to perform the indivisible function.

But in order rightly to grasp the nature of prophetic existence, the purpose of prophecy must also be considered.

Both, the Greek word of the oracle and the Biblical *nabi*-word, are bound to the situation. But the oracle answers to a situation brought before it as question by emissaries seeking information; the *nabi* sent by God speaks unquestioned into the biographical or historical situation. The answer of the oracle is the foretelling of an unalterable future, the appeal of the prophet means the openness and the deciding power of the hour. There the future is written on a scroll whose unrolling makes up the happening of history; here nothing is fixed or set down. Over the freely oscillating responses of man to the events that approach him, God mysteriously holds his sheltering hands: His power, which is greater and more mysterious than the formal "omnipotence" of dogma, can spare some real power for the moment of the creature.

In Herodotus (I.91) the Pythia proclaims that it is impossible even for a god to evade the destined fate. The paradigmatic book of Jonah relates that through a *nabi* God had destruction announced to the sinful city of Nineveh, not a conditional and preventable one: "Another forty days and Nineveh will be destroyed!" goes the prophetic cry,* but Nineveh accomplished the turning, and now God too "turned." This reciprocity of turning was the hidden meaning of the message, unknown (and later, when it became known, disagreeable) to the prophet himself. It is, therefore, a legitimate interpretation of the Biblical faith when the Jewish tradition reports of the prophets that they

* Jonah 3, 4.

159

had prophesied "only to those who turn." * The *nabi* speaks to the man in a situation of this man's present power of decision. His speech is not merely related to the situation. Its tie with the situation reaches unto the secret ground of creation in which existence is rooted. And just because it thus means the situation and corresponds to it, it remains valid for all generations and for all nations.

Prophecy is grounded in the reality of history as it is happening. Against all mantic historiosophy, against all certain knowledge of the future, whether of a dialectical or gnostic origin, there stands here the insight into the genuine existence of the happening moment, the moment so manifoldly determined and yet itself, in the simplicity of its decisions, really determining.

But the spoken word cannot alone satisfy the deciding power of the moment. In order to be equal to it, in order to meet it in its unreduced reality, the word needs to be supplemented by the power of signifying attitude and action. Only together with them can it present and invoke the power of decision. Not the word by itself has effect on reality, only the word that is set into the whole human existence, manifested from the whole, accompanying the whole.

In the Bible a sign can be understood as a proof or a corroboration; in its nature it is neither. One example out of many may show this. To the protest of Moses, "Who am I that I should go to Pharaoh, / that I should lead the sons of Israel out of Egypt!" God answers

* Babylonian Talmud, *Tractate Berachot* 34 b.

(Exodus 3:12): "Certainly, I will be with you, / and this is the sign that I myself send you: / when you have led the people out of Egypt, / you shall serve God on this mountain." This "sign" cannot be understood as a confirmation. But in the Bible a sign means, in fact, something else: embodiment. The Biblical man, and with him the Biblical God, desires that the spirit express itself more fully, more characteristically than in the word, that it embody itself. When this desire is expressed from man to God, it means, in Biblical language: to demand a sign, hence to demand the embodiment of the message. When it is expressed from God to man, it means to "tempt" a man, hence to draw forth from him what is hidden in him, to bring it to actuality; thus God tempts Abraham (Genesis 22) in that, merciful and terrible, he presents to his inner devotion the uttermost possibility of embodiment. But God also wills that man ask of Him the embodiment of the spirit; he who demands a sign of Him is confirmed; he who will not accept a sign that He offers manifests thereby not faith but lack of faith (Isaiah 7:11–13). The mission given to Moses out of the burning bush embodies itself in the "sign," when the people who have been led out of slavery in Egypt have come to the burning mountain * and now can serve the God who has brought them unto Himself "on eagles' wings" (Exodus 19:4).

The sign cannot be translated, cannot be replaced by a word; one cannot look up in a book of signs what

---

* In the Hebrew there is an untranslatable word-play on *sene*, thornbush, and Sinai.

a sign means. But the spoken word is perfected to its corporeality in the sign. The spoken word itself belongs to it, but just in its spokenness: as part of a bodily attitude and action.

Only what is transitory can become a simile. Both, sign and simile, are insoluble; out of both no statement can be made, both express what cannot be expressed in any other way—body and image do not let themselves be paraphrased; body, like image, first gives the *depth* of the word; and a bodily sign is no proof as the image-simile is no comparison.

The prophesying of the *nabi*, which is no soothsaying, but its exact opposite, has in view an event whose occurrence or non-occurrence depends upon the either-or of the moment. But events intended in this manner can only be adequately expressed through a sign-happening. The moment's fullness and power of decision can only be done justice to as an origin of happening through a sign-happening, a "symbolic act."

It is on this basis that all those sign-actions of the Biblical prophets are to be understood, from the most fleeting ones, as when Jeremiah breaks in pieces a water jug before the elders, or Ezekiel joins together two sticks of wood, to those that penetrate so far into life as when Hosea marries a strumpet and gives the children of this marriage ill-boding names. From an unsurpassably harsh example, like this last one, it becomes immediately clear that what is in question is not a practical metaphor but a bodily representation in the most exact sense of the term. What is here represented in the human world is the marriage between God and the whore Israel. "Go hence," speaks the voice in its first proclamation to the *nabi,* "take unto yourself a whore as a wife and children of whoredom, / *for* the country, whoring, whores away from following the Lord." This "for" tells in unsurpassably harsh manner how the lived life of the proclaimer whom God has summoned is claimed by Him as a sign, as a bodily representation of an experience of God, His experience with Israel. It is holy action of a dreadful seriousness, it is a real sacral drama that takes place here. The account of the marriage and the immediate identification with God's word intermesh with one another, awakening terror. Just reported was the name-giving of the "children of whoredom," that is, the children of the marriage of Hosea and the strumpet—"You-will-not-find-mercy" one daughter is named ("*for* I will no longer have mercy / on the House of Israel / that I should again be deceived by them, deceived"), "Not-my-people" a son is named ("*for* you are not my people, / and I am not there for you")—then there the voice of God suddenly (2:4) addresses in these children the children of Israel: "Attack your mother, attack! / For she is not my wife / and I am not her husband! / She must remove her whore's paint / from her face, / her prostitute's paint from / between her breasts!" We are here made to see most keenly into what depths of reality the existence of the "sign" penetrates.

The *nabi* does not merely act out a sign, he lives it. Not what he does is ultimately the sign, but while he does it he himself is the sign.

But the symbolical existence of the prophets attains

163

its highest intensity and clarity alike in Isaiah (8:11–22). It is a time of great confusion in which the future catastrophe of the people announces itself; truth and falsehood are so intermingled that the soul is barely still able to distinguish them, barely still able to recognize what is the right; God Himself is mistaken, misunderstood, misused, "as a snare and as a trap / for the settler in Jerusalem." Certainly there is also for this situation, pointing beyond the coming catastrophe, a comforting proclamation (it is found in our book of Isaiah, chapter 9:1–6). But to utter this now means to surrender it too to being mistaken, misunderstood, misused. Therefore, Isaiah says, as the word of the hour (8:15): "It is necessary to tie up the testimony / to seal up the instruction / in my disciples." As one ties up and seals a document, so does he with the proclamation which he delivers to his disciples: they themselves now represent the sealed document whose seal shall only be broken when, in the midst of catastrophe, the cry goes forth to the people which has run in vain to the oracle of its "chirping, muttering" "elves" (v. 19): "To the instruction! / to the testimony!" (v. 20). At that time, when the God who now "hides His face from the House of Jacob" (v. 17), will have mercy on "the remnant" that turns to Him, the prophet will "tarry" in the approaching "dread and darkening" (v. 22), in the midst of the crowd "who have no dawn" (v. 20), he and his "pupils" and his bodily children, to one of whom he has, clearly at God's command, given the prophetic name, "the remnant turns." And this tarrying he expresses thus (v. 18): "Now then!, / I and the children that the Lord has given me / are present in Israel for a sign and a confirmation, / by the Lord of hosts, / who dwells on Mount Zion." These men, the core of that "holy remnant," are present as signs; they live their independent lives at the same time as signs. This wholly signifying man (who is with the whole of his being a sign) is the "mouth of God." Through his symbolic existence is said what must now be said. That is something different from much that we call symbol. But no symbol, in no timeless height, can ever attain and again attain reality otherwise than by becoming embodied in such a human existence.

## II SACRAMENTAL EXISTENCE IN THE WORLD OF HASIDISM

A symbol is an appearance of meaning, the appearing and becoming apparent of meaning in the form of corporeality. The covenant of the Absolute with the concrete manifests itself in the symbol. But a sacrament is the binding of meaning to the body, fulfillment of binding, of becoming bound. The covenant of the Absolute with the concrete takes place in the sacrament.

Appearance, grasped as event, has a single direction; it goes from "above" to "below," that which appears enters into the corporeality that bears it. Binding has a twofold direction, what is above binds itself to what is below and what is below binds itself to what is above,

what is above binds what is below and what is below
binds what is above; they bind themselves to each
other, meaning and body bind each other. Where the
covenant manifests itself, it is like the reflected image
of a person himself out of sight; where the covenant
takes place, it is like "hand in hand." Hand in hand the
covenant is made, and hand in hand it is renewed.

That the divine and the human join with each other
without merging with each other, a lived beyond-tran-
scendence-and-immanence, is the foremost significance
of sacrament. But even when it is only two human
beings who consecrate themselves to each other sac-
ramentally—in marriage, in brotherhood—that other
covenant, the covenant between the Absolute and the
concrete, is secretly consummated; for the consecration does not come from the power of the human part-
ners, but from the eternal wings that overshadow both.
Everything unconditional into which men enter with
each other receives its strength from the presence of
the unconditional.

The sacrament has rightly been called "the most dynamic of all ritual forms." * But what is of greatest
importance in its dynamic is that it is stripped of its
essential character when it no longer includes an elementary, life-claiming and life-determining experience
of the *other,* the otherness, as of something coming to
meet one and acting toward one. That man in the
sacramental consecration neither merely "celebrates"
something, nor, still less, merely "experiences" something, that he is seized and claimed in the core of his

* R. R. Marett, *Sacraments of Simple Folk* (Oxford 1933), p. 9.

wholeness and needs nothing less than his wholeness
in order to endure it—that is what constitutes the three-
dimensionality of the occurrence, the reality of its
depth dimension. The ecclesiastical, or other similar
sacral conventions, levels the event down to a gesture,
while the mystic exaltation compresses it to an exuber-
antly heartfelt point.

All sacraments have a natural activity, an activity
taken from the natural course of life, that is consecrated
in them, and a material or corporeal otherness with
which one comes in holy contact—in a contact in which
its secret strength works on one.

"Primitive" man is a naïve pansacramentalist. Everything, to him, is full of sacramental substance, all, each
thing and each function, is ever ready to flash up as a
sacrament for him. He knows no selection of objects
and activities, only the methods and the favorable
hours. "It" is everywhere, one must only be able to
catch it. For this there are, to be sure, rules and
rhythms, but even these one only acquires when one
risks oneself therein, and he who is already capable of
knowing must expose himself ever anew to the danger-
ously seizing and claiming contact.

The crisis of all primitive humanity is the discovery
of the fundamentally not-holy, the a-sacramental, that
which withstands the methods and which has no
"hour," a province that steadily enlarges itself. In some
tribal communities, which we are still accustomed to
call primitive, one can observe, even if at times only
in single, peripheral individuals, this critical phase in
which the world threatens to become neutralized and

to deny itself the holy contact. This, for example, is what the Ba-ila of Northern Rhodesia may mean when they say about their God: "Leza has grown old" or "Leza is today no longer what he should be." * What we call religion in the narrower sense has perhaps arisen at one time and another in such a crisis. All historical religion is *selection* of sacramental material and actions. Through the separation of the holy from the abandoned profane, the sacrament is saved. The consecration of the binding becomes objectively-functionally concentrated.

But the sacrament thereby enters into a new and more difficult problematic. For a concrete religion can only authenticate the reality-seriousness of its concern if it exacts of the faithful not less than the involvement of the whole being of the person in his "faith." But the concentrated force of the sacrament that is founded on the separation of the holy from the profane easily misleads the faithful into feeling secure in a merely "objective" consummation without personal devotion, an *opus operatum*, and to evade being seized and claimed in his whole being. But to the extent that the life-substance of the faithful ceases to accrue to it, the sacrament loses in depth, in three-dimensional reality, in corporeality. Thus, perhaps, when in the sacramental sacrifice of Biblical Israel the central intention of offering oneself, in which one may only just let himself be represented by the animal, fades before the security of objectively performed ritual atone-

* E. W. Smith and A. M. Dale, *The Ila-Speaking Peoples of Northern Rhodesia,* II, 200 f.

ment.* Or when the Biblical anointing of the king, which placed him who was entrusted with the enduring task of being God's vice-regent in the living responsibility for this task †, degenerated in the Western coronation rites into a grandiose affirmation of personal power.

Where the inner crisis of a sacramentalism calls in question the original content of a religion, the original reality-seriousness of its concern, an attempt at reestablishing, at reformation may thrive. It too wills to rescue the consecration of the covenant: in that it takes seriously once again the presence of the human being. (In the strife between Luther and Zwingli over the nature of the divine presence in the Holy Communion, the presence of the human was also secretly in question; Luther perceived, Zwingli overlooked: that by a merely symbolic divine presence man is not seized and claimed in his whole presence.)

The principle of the selection of sacramental material and actions is not thereby attacked by reformations; only sectarians at times shake it without succeeding in overcoming and replacing it. It seems as though the man who has passed through the discovery of the fundamentally not-holy can no longer attain a holy relationship to the whole world, as though the reduction of the life of faith to one sphere is the unsurrenderable center of all religion because to surrender it means to pull down the bulwark against pantheism, which threatens concrete religion with dissolution. "Existing

* Cf. Buber, *Königtum Gottes*, p. 83 ff.
† Cf. my *The Prophetic Faith* (Macmillan, 1949), pp. 60–70.

169

alone," says the South Sea singer about his God Taaroa or Tangaroa, "he transforms himself into world. The pivots on which it turns is Taaroa, he is its supporting blocks, Taaroa is the sand of the primal grains." *
Concrete religion must fear letting the image of the Lord, the eternal partner of the religion of faith, run out into the sand of the primal grains.

But there has been one great religious movement, reformative in its core, that has projected a new pansacramentalism. Not a going back behind that critical discovery—the way there is barred and he who attempts to go back ends in madness or in mere literature —but a pressing forward to a new comprehensiveness. This unreduced comprehensiveness knows that the sacramental substance cannot be found or manipulated in the totality of things and functions, but it believes that it can be awakened and liberated in each object and in each action—not through any methods that one can somehow acquire but through the fulfilling presentness of the whole, wholly devoted man, through sacramental existence.

The great movement of which I speak, the Hasidic, must be taken up into the history of religion as an incomparable attempt to rescue the sacramental life of man from the corruption of the facile and the familiar.

For Hasidic pansacramentalism the holy in things is not, as for the primitive, a power which one takes possession of, a force which one can master, but it is laid

---

* I. A. Morenhout, *Voyages aux îles du Grand Océan* (Paris 1837) I 419. (The translation of Bastian in his "Heiligen Sage der Polynesier" is all too free.)

in the things as sparks and awaits the liberation and fulfillment of the man who gives himself completely. The man of sacramental existence is no magician; he does not merely stake himself in it, he really and simply gives himself; he exercises no power but a service, *the* service. He gives himself in service; that means: every time anew. To the question what (in the sacramental sense) is important, the answer was given: "What one is engaged in at the moment." But the actual, when it is taken seriously in its actuality, its uniqueness, its entering into the measure of the situation, shows itself as what cannot be anticipated, what is withdrawn from foresight. To the man of sacramental existence no kind of acquired rules and rhythms, no inherited methods of working avail, nothing "known," nothing "learned"; he has to withstand ever again the unforeseen, unforeseeable moment, ever again to extend liberation, fulfillment to a thing or being that he meets in the moment flowing toward him. And he can undertake no selection, no separation; for it is not for him to determine what has to meet him and what not. The not-holy, in fact, does not exist; there exists only the not yet hallowed, that which has not yet been liberated to its holiness, that which he shall hallow.

The Hasidic movement is customarily understood as the revolt of "feeling" against a religious rationalism that overemphasizes and ossifies the teaching of the divine transcendence, and against a ritualism that makes the practice of fulfilling the commands self-sufficient, and shallow. But what acts in this antithesis

cannot be grasped by the concept of feelings; it is the
soaring up of a genuine vision of unity and a passionate
demand for wholeness. What enters into battle here is
not simply a suppressed life-feeling that demands its
right, rather an image of God that has become greater
and a will to realization that has become stronger. That
double growth is no longer satisfied by the boundary
drawn in the teaching between God and the world and
the boundary drawn in life between the holy and the
profane. Both boundaries are static, fixed, timeless.
Both allow the currently real happening no influence.
The image of God that has become greater demands a
more dynamic, labile boundary between God and the
world, for it means a knowledge of a strength willing
to flow forth and yet self-limiting, of a resisting and
yet also yielding substance. And the will to realization
that has grown greater demands a more dynamic, labile
boundary between the holy and the profane spheres,
for it cannot concede that the redemption, in which the
unification of both spheres is promised, belongs by
nature only to the Messianic age; it must actively
accord the moment whatever can legitimately fall to
it. With all this, to be sure, one must still take into
consideration historically that already there, in that
"rabbinical" world around which the battle raged, all
the elements of the "new" were living, wrestling for
mastery and gaining ground. In order to understand
this one must know what has been all too little recognized: that in Judaism a tendency to sacramental life
has always been powerful. The fact—which can be
proved against other views—that there is hardly a

Christian sacrament that has not had a sacramental or semisacramental Jewish antecedent is not decisive here. But what is decisive is that always, even in the Talmudic period, masters of an unmistakably sacramental form of existence appear, men, therefore, in whose existence, in whose whole life-attitude, in whose experiences and actions the consecration of the covenant is present and fully operative. The historical series of such persons is well-nigh uninterrupted. The zaddik of the early period of Hasidism, the classic zaddik, is only an especially clear, theoretically delineated stamp of the same archetype, originating in the Biblical world and pointing into a future one.

But Hasidic pansacramentalism can be grasped at a still more significant level of being when one considers the relationship of the movement to the Kabbala.* Hasidism did not fight the Kabbala, like rabbinism; it wanted to continue and complete it; it has taken over its conceptions, in many cases its style, and in some even its method of teaching; and the Kabbalistic works of Hasidic authors do not stray from the tracks of the late Kabbala. Even theurgic practices of a Kabbalistic stamp frequently come to the surface in the history of Hasidism, at times in a wonderfully anachronistic manner. Nonetheless, in its own nature, in its actuality, it breaks with the basic principles of the Kabbala. Where it discusses its true object, life lived in the covenant, it speaks with quite a different voice, and in

* The authoritative work on the Kabbala is Gershom Scholem's *Major Trends in Jewish Mysticism* (2nd Edition, 1946).

essential points in an—never expressed, perhaps never conscious, and yet clear—opposition to the Kabbalistic teaching and attitude. And what weighs still more heavily: in a literature of legends, the like of which in compass, manysidedness, vitality, and popular wild charm I do not know,* what Hasidism has to tell of its central men, of all the many zaddikim, is almost entirely of a wholly other nature, a wholly other existence than that of Kabbalism, open to the world, pious toward the world, in love with the world.

An antithesis, first of all, that appears external but is significant: the Kabbala is esoteric. What it says hides what is not said. What is ultimately meant is only disclosed to the knowing, the initiated. Even as regards the approach to the reality of God a cleft runs through mankind. This Hasidism cannot tolerate: *here*, at the approach, there must not be any further differentiation, here stands the brotherhood of the sons of the Father, the mystery is valid for all or none, to none or all the heart of eternity is open. What is reserved for a knowing segment of mankind, what is withheld from the simple, cannot be the living truth. The Hasidic legend praises in bold, loving tones the simple man. He has a united soul; where unity of the soul is, there will God's unity dwell. Sacarmental covenant means the life of the unity with the unity.

The Kabbala, according to its origin but also according to its nature which ever again breaks through, is

* A comprehensive selection is offered by my book *Tales of the Hasidim—The Early Masters* (1947), *The Later Masters* (1948).

a gnosis, and, to be sure, in contradistinction to all others,\* an antidualistic one.

The origin of all gnosis—to express it with the simplification necessary in this connection—is the primal question, intensified to despair of the world. How is the contradiction which in every course of life and history is experienced as insuperable, the corroding essence of existence in the world, to be reconciled with the being of God? This intensification of the question is later than the Old Testament; every true gnosis originates in a cultural sphere that has been touched by the Old Testament, almost every one as a, directly or indirectly expressed, rebellion against it. The Biblical experience of unity—one decisive power, a superior partner of man—met the experience of contradiction that announced itself out of painful depths by pointing to the hiddenness of the mystery: the determination of what appears as contradiction or absurdity is an insurmountable barrier for knowledge (Job), but dimly perceivable in the lived mystery of suffering (Deutero-Isaiah); just here arises the strongest expression of

---

\* That the teaching of Plotinus is also to be regarded as a predominantly dualistic transformation of gnosis will be shown in the concluding volume of Hans Jonas's important work, *Gnosis und spätantiker Geist* [Two volumes have already been published. The third will appear in 1961 as Teil II, zweite Hälfte—*Die philosophische-mystische Gnosis*—Ed.], but it can always only be regarded as a metamorphosis of gnosis into philosophy and never, like the Kabbala, as gnosis. [Some indications of the relation between Plotinus and gnosis are available to the English-speaking reader in Hans Jonas's *The Gnostic Religion. The Message of the Alien God and the Beginnings of Christianity* (Boston: Beacon Press, 1958). Cf. pp. xvii, 61, 162 ff., 251, 286.—Ed.]

sacramental existence in which the suffering itself becomes a sacrament (Isaiah 53). But the Jewish apocalyptic literature no longer mastered the question; the *Apocalypse of Esdras* ("The Fourth Book of Esdras") no longer knows the faithful intercourse with the mystery, but retains only the submission without nearness, which is at the same time the renunciation of the world, the dwindling away of the sacramental life. It is at this point that gnosis intervenes, employing the stones of the ruined giant edifices of the ancient Oriental religions for the most fantastic new structure. It explains the problematic of the world as a problematic of the divinity: whether it be that an evil or merely bad negative principle stands in opposition to the good God, or whether it be that from the good itself arise fragile or corruptible powers that fall into the spheres of evil and as world-soul bear the fate of the contradiction until they are allowed to ascend again. In these systems the Other, the antagonistic or merely resisting, the counter-power or the counter-world, is always presupposed, more or less massively described, sometimes only just as "spaces of shadows and the emptiness" (Valentinus). To take from this Other its independence, to include it too in the dynamic of the divine unity, is the undertaking of the Kabbala.

The Kabbala, employing a combination of gnostic and Neo-Platonic schemata, fashioned a Talmudic teaching into a monstrous prodigy. It is, in opposition to the apocalyptic resignation, the teaching of the divine attributes or essences of severity and mercy and their dialectical intercourse in which the drama of the world process appears as one taking place within the deity. This dual dialectic, which must be understood as real and yet not dualistic, is diversified by the Kabbala in the intercourse with one another of the *sefirot,* the divine primal numbers or primal splendors, the powers and orders which it sees as coming forth from the eternally hidden aseity of God, which is called the "Without Limit," * through a "contraction" and a "separation," remaining in God and yet founding the world. Their stages of descent continue into the world levels till in the lowest, the corporeal world of "shells"; the dynamic of their coverings and uncoverings, pourings forth and dammings up, bindings and loosenings, engenders the problematic of cosmic and creaturely beings. Like the pre-cosmic catastrophes of the "Death of the Primal Kings" or the "Breaking of the Vessels" with their cosmic consequences, so too all innerworldly hindrances and disturbances, down to the demonic powers that attack the human soul, proceed from untyings, displacements of weight, overflowings in the realm of the aeons. And yet it is just from the base of this our world that the overcoming of the problematic can be effected: through the sacramental deed of the man who praying and acting intends the elemental mystery of the names of God and their intertwining, service is rendered toward the unification of the divine forces, in which the second, the perfect unity of existing being prepares itself. The Kabbalistic reconciliation of the experience of unity and the ex-

* In Hebrew *En Sof* or *Hin Sof.*—Ed.

177

perience of contradiction is also ultimately, like the Biblical, a sacramental one.

But the protest against the Kabbala, unexpressed yet strong in its factuality, announces itself in twofold fashion in Hasidism.

The one protest is directed against the schematization of the mystery. Central to the Kabbala, as to all gnosis, is seeing through the contradiction of being and removing itself from it. Central to Hasidism is faithfully to endure the contradiction and thus to redeem the contradiction itself. The Kabbala draws a map of the primal mysteries in which the origins of the contradiction also have their place. Hasidism, in so far as it—frequently, but seldom other than peripherally—"pursues Kabbala," may preserve the Kabbala's image of the upper world simply because it is not able to replace it by any other. But in its own sphere Hasidism is agnostic; it is not concerned with objective knowledge that can be formulated and schematized, but with vital knowledge, with the Biblical "knowing" in the reciprocity of the essential relation to God. Certainly, "just the classic masters of the Kabbala attacked the tendency to regard the unfolding into finiteness of the goodness lying in God (presented in their teaching as combining theology and cosmogony until the two become indistinguishable) as an objective process, that is a process as it appears from the side of God." *
But that is only a bracketed metaphysical-epistemological thesis with no tendency toward practice; it no-

* Gershom Scholem, article "Kabbala" in the *Encyclopaedia Judaica* IX.

where enters into the system. The whole systematic structure of the Kabbala is determined by the principle of a certitude that almost never stops short, almost never shudders, almost never prostrates itself. In contrast, it is precisely in stopping short, in letting itself be disconcerted, in deep knowledge of the impotence of all "information," of the incongruence of all possessed truth, in the "holy insecurity," that Hasidic piety has its true life. In it too is founded its love of the "ignorant man." What is of importance? One may "clamber about in the upper worlds"—suddenly it touches him and all is blown away, and in infinite, pathless darkness one stands before the eternal presence. Only the defenseless outstretched hand of the insecure is not withered by the lightning. We are sent into the world of contradiction; if we soar up away from it into spheres where this world seems translucent to us, we foresake our mission. It would be contrary to the faith and humor of our existence (Hasidism is both faithful and humorous) to suppose that there is a level of being into which we only need to lift ourselves in order to get "behind" the problematic. The absurd is given to me that I may endure and sustain it with my life; this, the enduring and sustaining of the absurd, is the meaning which I can experience.

The other Hasidic protest against the Kabbala turns against the magicizing of the mystery. Magic is not at all identical with faith in the transcendent working of man, that is in the influence of the human being and human life beyond the realm that can be comprehended by causality and logic; rather it is, within this

179

faith, the belief that there are certain transmittable and transmitted inner and outer actions and attitudes through the execution of which the believed-in effect is obtained. Magic (which can exist inside as well as outside of sacramentalism) is thus, where it appears joined with gnosis, simply its other side: the ability to survey the means—here the means employed against the contradiction of being—belongs together with the gnostic ability to see through the contradiction. In the Kabbala these transmitted magical methods can be applied in conjunction with quite varied life activities; it is the *kavanot,* the intentions, which were drawn from the rich store of name- and letter-mysticism and which, together with their influence on letters and names, wants to have an effect on the entities themselves.

And again, as in its teaching Hasidism at its periphery preserves but at its center neglects the Kabbalistic-gnostic schemata, so in its practice it still knows, certainly, of the methods of intention that can be learned—all kinds of Kabbalistic-magical material down to saving formulae and amulets; but its character asserted itself in factual, not seldom too in programmatic, opposition to it. Against the knowable *kavanot*—in such and such a way one is to meditate, on this and this one is to reflect—there arose the one life-embracing *kavana* of the man devoted to God and His work of redemption. As Hasidism strove to overcome the separation between the holy and the profane, so it also strove to overcome the emphasis on fixed procedures of intention from out of the fullness of the living act. Not by accompanying any action with an already known mystical method but by performing this action with the whole of his being directed toward God does a man practice *kavana* in truth. What can be known in advance is not suited to give the central content of the deed; for it is not with arbitrariness posing as originality but in connection with what approaches us that the sacramental deed is to be done—as our counter-movement. But what approaches us cannot be known beforehand; God and the moment cannot be known beforehand; and the moment is God's moment; therefore, we can, indeed, prepare ourselves ever again for the deed, but we cannot prepare the deed itself. The substance of the deed is ever again given to us; rather, it is offered us: through that which happens to us, which meets us—through everything which meets us. Everything wants to be hallowed, to be brought into the holy, everything worldly in its worldliness: it does not want to be stripped of its worldliness, it wants to be brought in its worldliness into the *kavana* of the redemption—everything wants to become sacrament. The creature, the things seek us out on our paths; what comes to meet us on our way needs us for its way. "With the floor and the bench" shall one pray *; they want to come to us, everything wants to come to us, everything wants to come to God through us. What concern of ours, if they exist, are the upper worlds! Our concern is "in this lower world, the world of corporeality, to let the hidden life of God shine forth."

* Buber, *Tales of the Hasidim,* I (1947), p. 269.

# CHAPTER VI

# GOD AND THE SOUL

I It is always questionable to try to define mysticism, or any other religious teaching, on the basis of its subject matter or first principle; one obtains then only a concept or thesis, at once abstract and somewhat vague, which fails to grasp just what makes mysticism a singular and remarkable special type of religious life. We do better if we proceed from the experience of the soul that is clearly common to all mystics since they all allude to it in some fashion, even if at times only in a veiled way or, indeed, in so objective an expression that the personal substratum, just that experience, does not come into our view; even there there are moments when the stern tone of objective statement is suddenly thrilled through by an overpowering memory. Now one may, indeed, call that experience an experience of unity; but we shall again have in our hands something abstract and vague if we think perhaps of a contemplation of unity in which, to be sure, the contemplating man recedes but his basic situation, which he to some extent still feels in the midst of his experience, the basic situation of all our human contemplation, remains: the division of being into a contemplating and a contemplated. One of the greatest among the mystics, Plotinus, has, in particular, given strong grounds for such a misunderstanding when, as a true Greek still in the late period of the fusion of all the elements of the spirit, he reported that experience in optical language, namely, in the image of the eye looking at light. Even in Plotinus it becomes clear to us on closer observation that this is only one, if also the thinnest, of the garments in which the mystical experience clothes itself, in order to be able to reveal itself, or rather in order to enable its bearer to fit what he experiences into the framework of his living and then into that of his knowing. In truth, the decisive factor within that experience is not yet that the multiplicity of manifestations collapses into the one, that the play of colors gives place to the unconditionality of white light. What is decisive is that the act of contemplating is obliterated in the contemplator; not the dissolution of the phenomenal multiplicity, but that of the constructive duality, the duality of experiencing I and experienced object, is the decisive factor, that which is peculiar to mysticism in the exact sense. And, mysticism in the exact sense can only be spoken of, to be sure, where it is not a question of men of an early dawn stage preceding the clear sundering of subject and object, but of those whose basic situation has become a matter of course: a self-enclosed I and over against it a self-enclosed world. This duality is a fundamental one even if only gradually recognized by the human spirit. That it is dissolved in certain moments of personal life in favor of an overpowering experience of unity is what awakens that ever-recurring deep astonishment that we rediscover in all mystics, even though in varying degrees of expression.

In all mysticism, however, that springs from the soil of the so-called "theistic" religions, there is an additional factor to which a special, specifically religious significance is to be accorded. Here the mystic knows of a close personal intercourse with God. This intercourse has as its goal, certainly, a union with God, a union that not seldom is felt and presented in images of earthly eros. But in erotic intercourse between being and being as in the intercourse between man and God it is still just the duality of these beings which is the elementary presupposition of what passes between them. It is not the duality of subject and object: neither is to the other a mere object of contemplation that does not itself participate in the relation. It is the duality of I and Thou, both entering into the reciprocity of the relation. No matter how absolute God is comprehended as being, He is here, nonetheless, not the whole but the Facing One. He is the One standing over against this man; He is what this man is not and is not what this man is. It is precisely on this duality that the longing for union can base itself. In other words, in this close intercourse that the mystic experiences, God, no matter how infinite he is comprehended as being, is still Person and remains Person. And even if the mystic wants to be merged in Him, he means none other than Him whom he knows in this intercourse, just this Person. The I of the mystic seeks to lose itself in the Thou of God, but this Thou of God, or, after the I of the mystic has been merged in Him, this absolute I of God, cannot pass away. The "I am" of man must vanish so that the "I am" of God alone remains. "Between me and thee," goes one of the sayings of al-Hallaj, the great martyr of Islamic mysticism, "there is an 'I am' that torments me. Ah! Through thy 'I am' take away my 'I am' from between us both." The mystic never thinks of calling into question the personal character of this divine "I am." "I call thee," says al-Hallaj, ". . . no, it is thou who callest me to thee! How could I have said to thee, 'It is thou,' if thou hadst not whispered to me, 'It is I.'" The I of the revealing God, the I of the God who grants to the mystic the intercourse with Him, and the I of God in which the human is merged are identical. In the realm of the intercourse with God the mystic remains what he was in the realm of revelation, a theist.

It is otherwise when mysticism, stepping beyond the realm of experienced intercourse, dares to deal with God as He is in Himself, that is, outside His relation to man, indeed outside His relationship to the created world. Certainly, it knows well that, as Meister Eckhart put it, no one can say of God what He is. But its conception of the absolute unity, a unity hence that nothing can any longer stand over against, is so strong that even the highest conception of the person must yield before it. The unity that is related to something other than itself is not the perfect unity; the perfect unity can no longer be personal. By this the

187

mysticism that has sprung from the soil of a theistic religion by no means wishes to deny the personal character of God; but it strives to raise that perfect unity, that nothing any longer stands over against, above even the God of revelation and to distinguish between the Godhead abiding in pure being and the active God. Perfect unity only *is*, it does not act. "Never has the Godhead," says Eckhart, "done this or that, but only God creates all things." There, to that primal being before creation, to that unity above all duality, the mystic ultimately strives to return; he wants to become as he was before creation.

Theistic mysticism does not always strain its conception of the unity to the extreme of setting up a duality in the very being of God. Islamic mysticism avoids doing that by seeking to raise the attribute of acting to an abstract height where it is compatible with the perfect unity; of course, it only apparently succeeds in doing this, namely, through dealing with the monotheistic tradition of the acting God, mystically transfigured, as it were, without anything of the activity of the active one penetrating into the mystical sphere itself—the activity of God is directed toward the world, His unity is essentially acosmic, the one manifests God's doings in the human community, the other only knows of Him in so far as He has contact with the soul; thus Islamic mysticism purchases a questionable unity of God at the price of a bifurcation of the religious life.

Christian mysticism, at the height of its theology, proceeds more boldly and consistently here. With unsurpassable trenchancy, it places the tension in the divine itself. "God and Godhead," says Eckhart, "are different as heaven and earth . . . God becomes and ceases to be." The divine, therefore, is here called "God" in so far as from perfect unity, which nothing stands over against, it has made itself in creation and revelation into the One facing the world and thereby into the partaker in its becoming and ceasing to be. For "God" only exists for a world, by the divine becoming just its God, the world's; when world becomes, God becomes, and if there is no world, God ceases to be, and again there is only Godhead.

It is already clear from this that it would be a grave error to ascribe to the mystic the view that the distinction between Godhead and God is only one of perspective, that is, that it does not exist in itself but only from the viewpoint of the world. Such a view would above all empty the historical revelation of reality. That is far from genuine theistic mysticism. It sees the distinction rather as one grounded in God's being itself and consummated by Him.

Thus far has Christian mysticism in Eckhart—as Indian mysticism before it in Sankara—pressed on; further it has not attempted to press. Yet by that an enigma that confronts us at the borderline of human being, there, where it comes in contact with the divine, has only been transposed into the divine being itself and thereby, for a time, withdrawn from further investigation. Not for ever; for in the history of later mysticism there is one more attempt, even if only a fragmentary one that appears to have come to a standstill at the start, to press still further and here too still to ask "Why?" The question can be provisionally formulated thus: Why has God become Person? Hasidism (and, so far as I can see, it alone) has undertaken to answer this question—or rather, as will be shown, a related one. This is attested by intimations of its greatest thinker, the Maggid of Mezritch, that we can extract and to some extent put together from the notes of disciples. Here is one of the few points in which Hasidic theology goes beyond the later Kabbala in whose footsteps here too it walks, even if only gropingly.

# II

The idea of a self-limitation of God in the primal act of creation is, as has been stated, a basic idea of the Kabbala. It follows of itself, as it were, when the concept of a creation of all things out of a "Nothing" standing over against God is replaced by the concept of an emanation of the worlds out of God. World, be it even the highest, is by its nature limited; it is limited, by the fact that, actually or potentially, there exists an other that it is not. But just for this reason the first act of emanation already limits God Himself. Certainly He remains in Himself the limitless, but in that now there is no longer merely Himself but also world, even if only in the form of the first primeval point, in that God in Himself makes the limited possible and actual, He limits Himself. Not, therefore, that He Himself has been or could be limited by world and worlds, since in Himself, indeed, He cannot be touched or circumscribed by any other; but through the fact that He has "left space for" the limited, He has now accomplished self-limitation there where the limited is, and in so far as it is. (Naturally what we here call unlimited and limited must not be confused with notions of spatial infinity and finitude since space as such is first established in creation; and similarly the use of terms of time, unavoidable in human speech when speaking of the act of creation, must not be taken to mean that creation occurred in time, which rather was first established by it: the self-limitation, in truth, does not proceed in time but in eternity.)

The motive given by the later Kabbala for the original act of divine self-limitation is, however, of great significance: There arises in God's will—as Chaim Vital expresses it in the famous opening of his "Tree of Life" —the desire to create the world in order to do good to His creatures. For God's kindness to actualize itself there must be something other than Himself, something outside Himself to which He can do good. Here we see clearly the fundamental difference from the teaching of Spinoza. Spinoza had to withhold all personality from God; the love of this God, in which His being of necessity culminated, could not be love for another but only the all-love of the Unlimited for itself. The Kabbala does not shrink from finding in the "Godhead" something that first attains its full effect only in the action of "God": the kindness; and for this effect there is need of an other who needs kindness. Already the "Godhead" wants to give Itself out of kind-

191

ness, it longs for a recipient for its "light." And so the self-limitation continues, for the world is not in a state to receive the fullness of the divine light, and "on account of His great love," as the Maggid of Mezritch says, God limits his illuminating power further. But even thus "Godhead" becomes "God," whereby in Hasidism, as already before it, just the former is designated by the Tetragrammaton, which is originally by far the more personal of the two names; ever more strongly there breaks through in Him pure "Being." "One receives the light of the sun only through a curtain," says the Maggid; "so one cannot receive the illuminating power of the 'Being' * except through Elohim." Even this is no new image; but it stands in a new connection that makes it new. The Godhead emanates a world in order to bring into operation that in itself which is person, the personal kindness, the personal will to give; and in order that this world might receive what It desires to give of itself, the Godhead becomes God for it altogether. The Maggid goes so far as to designate the self-limitation itself with the name "God" and, in the footsteps of the Kabbala, to explain the opening words of the Bible, "In the beginning created (He) God" as meaning that the Godhead has "in the beginning" transformed Itself into God.

If, however, according to the tradition of the secret teaching, the God working in nature, limiting Himself to it, is called Elohim, how are we then to understand

* The "Being," HaVaYaH, is here equated with YHVH, the "Being one" (traditionally spoken Adonai, that is, the Lord, and translated accordingly).

that the Bible designates the revealing God, the God acting in Israel, by the primal name of the Godhead, the Tetragrammaton? Not merely the creation—revelation too is a descent of the Godhead. But it is no real self-limitation: here works the God that has not entered into the world, the unlimited God, the bearer of the limitless light, the Godhead, the pure Being; and just It, the absolute Godhead, works as Person. To understand this one must bear in mind the significance that is ascribed within the creation of the world to the creation of man and within the human race to the people of Israel and within Israel to the zaddik.

That the worlds could not receive the limitless light and God therefore limited it, in no way means that He renounced attaining the recipient for it. To attain him, He created man, but man through his sin forfeits becoming the recipient of the limitless light. Now He lets Israel arise in the midst of the human race. In order to give it the light as word, "YHVH descends to Mount Sinai." This action out of love, says the Maggid of Mezritch, is, in fact, a descent of God. But what He reveals to the people of Israel as Torah, that is in its essence the limitless light itself. Israel pledges itself to Him, but it too could not receive the light truthfully and fully. Now God waits with His hidden limitless light for the recipient. God wants Israel to become zaddikim, that is, recipients, for "more than the calf wants to suck, the cow wants to suckle." For this reason God practices in each generation not a real but only an apparent and temporary limitation of illuminating power. He acts, in so doing, like a father who, in order that his small son may learn to understand him more and more, and at last completely, begins by seemingly limiting his own understanding and making himself a child for the sake of the child. This simile recurs in countless variants in the sayings of the Maggid which try to make clear how this second, pedagogical self-limitation is related to the first, cosmogonic one. And God's intention succeeds: the zaddik arises. He presses forward through all the worlds to God, receives His light, enters into the unity of His being. As a man the zaddik is what every man as such is, *dam*, blood, but because he cleaves to Him who is *alufo-shel-olam*, the prince of the world, and the divine principle is thus united with his blood, there comes from the letter *aleph* and the word *dam* for the first time truly Adam: the true man, the receiver of the limitless light, has arisen.

As we have seen, however, the distinction here is not, as in Indian and Christian mysticism, that between a super-personal, inactive Godhead and a personal, acting God, and yet we do not go back behind these; rather, out of the presuppositions of the Jewish tradition and in particular of the Kabbala we are led beyond them in a highly significant point. A distinction is effected within the divine working in that the self-imparting of God to His recipient, the revealing, is separated from all other, all natural working of God: He who imparts Himself is not Elohim, the God of the self-limitation whose act establishes the worlds, but the limitless primal Godhead itself. The imparting, to be sure, makes use of the limitation on its way until, henceforth freed from all need of limitation, it reaches its true recipient, but the self-imparting has not itself been limited, has not, as with Elohim, been transformed into world and worlds, but limiting its illuminating power from time to time in order to attain the recipient, it has still remained untransformed in itself without leaving any trace of the world on itself. We stand here before a paradoxical activity that does not impair the absoluteness of the original divine. The distinction is not here, as in the mysticism of Sankara and Eckhart, between a "Godhead" resting within itself and an active personal God, but almost the reverse, between the original Godhead designated by the Tetragrammaton, that wants to impart Himself directly, and in order to do this accomplishes the limitation to Elohim, the creation, and this other, Elohim, who in the entire fullness of nature in the widest sense, in all worlds, works what is worked, creates, animates, inspirits. The recipient of YHVH arises through Elohim; but it is YHVH Himself who leads him until he has truly become a recipient, and this leading is again nothing else than an imparting, indirect but becoming ever more direct. Of the two Elohim is the impersonal figure of God that may be compared, if one wishes, with Spinoza's *natura naturans;* but here there stands, before and above this, the original Godhead, the "Being," and it is both at once, the perfect unity and the limitless Person. *"Esse est Deus,"* says Eckhart, and that can be said here too, but here the Being includes the Person, namely the person in the paradoxical sense, the limitless, the absolute Person. Not the *tzimtzum*, the self-limitation, but the limitless original Godhead itself, the Being, speaks the "I" of revelation.

The question from which we set out, the question at which Indian and Christian mysticism have remained standing, and beyond which Hasidism has pressed further, is, accordingly, not to be formulated as we have done, to begin with, following the presuppositions of those two traditions. Rather it has split for us into a double question. The first runs somewhat as follows: "Why has the limitless Godhead become the limited God wandering through the worlds and performing the work of creation in His limitedness?" And the second: "Why has the limitless Godhead, from being an absolute Person, whom nothing stands over against, become one faced by a recipient?" To the first question the Kabbala gave the answer: From kindness. To the second Hasidism answers: From longing for the recipient upon whom It, the Godhead, could bestow its light. Both answers are one. The actuality of God's way is to be understood from the actuality of His will to show love.

From this position, that the limitless original Godhead itself is the God of revelation, is also to be understood a fundamental Hasidic view attaining expression with uttermost power of imagery in the sayings of the Maggid. This is a view that has not seldom been misunderstood as "pantheistic" (as generally, indeed, in the province of living religion such simplifying cate-

gories are for the most part misunderstandings). I mean
the view that has elaborated the presence of the living
God in us into a sensible completeness.* Man is visited
by the divine might or substance in two ways: as creature by the creative strength of Elohim which lends
him its strength, and as person by the settling down
of the Shekina which, when it comes, lifts him above
himself. The first kind is constitutive and enduring, the
second gracious and unforeseeable; if one can compare
the former to that underground water that soaks the
depths of the earth and from there keeps the soil moist
and fruitful, so one can compare the latter to the fruc-
tifying rain that "descends to earth and causes the
grain to grow." We are surrounded on all sides by the
creative strength of God that grasps and bears the creation; but we ourselves are also penetrated by it for it
has entered into creation: "We go in the Creator,
blessed be He, and without His outpouring and His
life-strength we can make no movement." Through
Him we live in the strictest sense, because He lives in
us: "God dwells in the midst of the limbs of man from
his head to the sole of the foot." What we do, we do
by the strength of God; only the use, the direction that
we make out of the divine strength lies within our
will; we can drag it down to the vulgar level, and we
can, mindful of its essence and origin, direct it up to
heaven. And if a man with the concentrated strength
of his soul turns himself to heaven and his mere crea-

* In the following passages I disregard the teaching of the
"sparks" which is a river-basin in itself and which is discussed
in other sections of this book.

turely strength does not suffice to bear the devotion of his whole self upward, then, as soon as he has said only, "Lord, open my lips," the Shekina, which sojourns in exile with us, clothes itself in him and itself speaks the words and in them soars upward to Her "Spouse." But here too we must keep clearly in mind that our human element should be equal to the communion with the Shekina and not pull Her down; for certainly it raises us in the word "from temple hall to temple hall," but in each one we are judged.

Here already it becomes clear that God demands what He demands of us not as Elohim, but as YHVH, hence in His original essence. The Godhead as the perfect unity, the God before and above creation, is at the same time the commanding God. For just He is the kind One who creates the worlds to actualize His kindness; He is the great lover who has set man in the world in order to be able to love him—but there is no perfect love without reciprocity, and He, the original God, accordingly longs that man should love Him. Everything follows from this, all teaching, all "morality," for in the innermost core nothing is wanted and nothing is demanded from above but love of God. Everything follows from this; for man cannot love God in truth without loving the world in which He has set His strength and over which His Shekina rests. People who love each other in holy love bring each other toward the love with which God loves His world.

In Hasidism—and in it alone, so far as I can see, in the history of the human spirit—mysticism has become *ethos.* Here the primal mystical unity in which the soul wants to be merged is no other form of God than the demander of the demand. Here the mystical soul cannot become real if it is not one with the moral.

# CHAPTER VII

# REDEMPTION

A unique event in world history is the phenomenon which appeared to us in the history of Judaism. The whole of the historical experience of a nation is there concentrated in the one fateful problem of exile and redemption. Out of this common experience of exile and redemption the nation was born. On the memory of this historical event, which the spiritual leaders of Israel had declared time and again to be the work of God with the nation and a covenant between the nation and God, is founded the connection between the past and the future which is living in the nation's consciousness in a way which is not to be found in any other nation.

During the period between the exile of the ten tribes and the exile of Judah, a conception of exile and redemption is developed by the prophets, according to which the redemption of humanity and its transformation into a kingdom of God is connected with the redemption of Israel and its transformation into a center of this kingdom.

## Redemption

At the time of the return from the Babylonian exile begins a spiritual process in which the sphere of Jewish faith is penetrated by ideas of cosmic and individual redemption stemming from the Eastern nations (especially Persia), and also from Greece, without these ideas at that period being incorporated completely in the traditional concept of the redemption of Israel. Such a complete blend starts only after the destruction of the Second Temple. It is mainly the Kabbala which combines these foreign elements (and with them the gnostic idea of the redemption of the Godhead itself) with the Jewish faith and brings them into the unity of a single system—the heart of which is the hope for the redemption of Israel. But the doctrine which was born as a result of this combination is "a secret teaching" which, by its nature, is for the time being known only to the few, those who "know" (the esoteric knowledge), and is unable to penetrate into the faith of the people. Only in Hasidism does the doctrine of redemption win the heart of the simple man, not only because it finds in Hasidism an expression but because here there is a special active task for every Jew in the redemption of the world.

Four kinds of exile and redemption converge in the doctrine of Hasidism: a) the exile of the "holy sparks" and their redemption, b) the exile of the individual and the redemption of the individual through the "transmigrations" of the individual soul and its transformation in this way into higher stages, c) national exile and national redemption, d) the exile of the Shekina and its redemption. These four kinds are interconnected in a particular way, namely, there are certain relations between the exile of the nation and its redemption, on one hand, and the exile of any of the other kinds, on the other hand. Thus there are those, for example, who believe the goal of the exile of Israel to lie in the fact that the nation of Israel is destined to uplift the "sparks" which have been dispersed throughout the world, or who see in the uplifting of individual souls a condition for the redemption of Israel. This connection between the national redemption and all the other kinds of redemption is sometimes so strong that the exile of the Shekina is not only seen as parallel to the exile of Israel, but the redemption of the Shekina is described in the same images and expressions as those used for the description of the redemption of "Knesset Israel," the congregation of Israel. The exile of the nation is connected by a very strong tie with the exile of the world, and the redemption of the nation with the redemption of the individual soul. Both the exile of the nation and its redemption are to be thought of not by themselves, but only in relation to the destiny of the world and to the destiny of the soul.

The exile of Israel is not merely a historical-national fact; its causes are connected with the deepest elements of God's sorrow, caused by the creation which He has created. The redemption of Israel is not an isolated goal toward which to aspire; it depends on the correction of the error which has penetrated into the very roots of creation. The national element is central in the Hasidic faith, but this element has no existence without the other elements whose center it is; on the contrary, it does not exist except as it serves as their center and only in so far as it serves as their center.

From this standpoint it may also be understood why Hasidism has produced what it has produced in just this way and not in any other. The teaching of redemption which existed in it was so great that Hasidism could have developed into one of the great religions of redemption in the world, but the central importance of the national element has prevented it. Hasidism could not become the property of the whole of humanity because it could not aspire to the redemption of the world as the essential thing and to the redemption of Israel as merely a tiny part of the great redemption. It could not pass to humanity because it could not disconnect the redemption of the soul from the redemption of the nation.

The action of Christianity at the time of her separation from Judaism, her forsaking of the idea of the holiness of the nation and the absolute value of its task, could not be imitated by Hasidism, for, in the eyes of Hasidism, between the world and the individual there is an intermediate existence which cannot be overlooked—the nation. The kingdom of God in the eyes of Christianity means the establishment of God's Kingship over redeemed souls in the world, in which there is no longer a relation between the nation as a nation and God; therefore, people became Christians only as individuals, but the nations as nations remained idol worshippers, and as long as nations exist, the world will not become Christian. In the eyes of Hasidism, in contrast, the kingdom of God has remained the same as it always was in the eyes of Judaism—to which Hasidism has remained faithful willingly and unwillingly—namely the establishment of the kingship of God over the "human nation" as a nation of nations, a nation consisting of nations; and this kingdom will not come about until one nation, which has been destined for this purpose, shall begin to establish in its own way of living the will of God for the redemption of the world. Certainly this does not mean the weakening of the national existence, and of course not its abolition, but on the contrary—its decisive concentration. Therefore Hasidism announced with great enthusiasm that Israel, the heart of humanity, and Eretz * Israel, the heart of the world, are required by each other, and without their unity redemption will not come.†

I want to show now how in Hasidism the national element was combined with the cosmic element, with the individual element, with the religious element, and how they became a real unity, according to the order of these four kinds of exile and redemption. I shall illustrate with passages from Hasidic literature.

The connection between the national and the cosmic element can be stated thus: the exile of Israel is connected with the exile of the holy sparks which exist in all things and its redemption is connected with their redemption. "The main purpose of the exile," says

* The land of Israel, i.e., Palestine—Ed.
† Cf. Martin Buber, *Israel and Palestine. The History of an Idea* (New York: Farrar, Straus, and Young, 1953; London: East and West Library, 1952), pp. 89–91, 102–108.—Ed.

*Redemption*

Rabbi Nachman of Bratslav, the great-grandson of the Baal-Shem, "is to gather the 'discarded ones,' who are the sparks that were discarded into the 'shells' of the *kelipot,* as it is said, 'Israel was exiled for the sake of winning proselytes.' In a way it is hard to understand the exile, which is supposed to be in order that Israel— who has transgressed in Eretz Israel—should be purified and return to God, blessed be His name, for this is a very difficult problem: If in the place of our life and holiness which is in Eretz Israel, the *'Yetzer-Hara'* (evil urge) has overwhelmed Israel and made them sin, how will there be any hope in places outside of Eretz Israel where the atmosphere is profane? Will Israel repent and be made perfect there? But the truth is that all this . . . all these ups and downs happen to every one of Israel according to his type and stage, so that there are some who have fallen into the depths of the abyss. Because God, blessed be His name, thinks thoughts so that nobody will be discarded before Him. Because, in truth, sometimes exactly when a person arrives at a very low place far away from holiness, exactly there he may be awakened in a great awakening toward God, blessed be His name, and there are many motives and variations for it." And the Baal-Shem-Tov himself says: "This is a very great rule that a man is benefited by the life that is in everything that he wears and eats and even in the tools that he uses; in them are the holy 'sparks' that belong to the 'root' of his soul; when he uses this tool or when he eats food even for the needs of his body, he brings salvation to these 'sparks.'" "Therefore, one should have mercy on his

207

tools and all his possessions for the sake of the sparks that are in them." It means that he has to deal with all things in holiness. And the great disciple of the Baal-Shem-Tov, Rabbi Dov Baer, the Maggid of Mezritch, adds and explains: "Even by eating and drinking in purity and holiness, it is possible to hasten the coming of redemption, because through the *kavanot,* the intentions of eating, it is possible to remove the precious from the worthless, thus emptying the 'Other Side' * of the holy sparks that have remained in it." The destiny and task of the nation are therefore interconnected, and each and every one among the people of the nation has a part in its task, just as he shares its destiny.

Just as the sparks are in exile, so also the souls of the people. Their transmigrations from lower to higher stages are merely a result of the soul's aspiration to reach perfection. And here, too, the exile and redemption of the nation are connected in their depth with those of the soul. The exile of Israel is meant for the purification of the souls, which helps them to ascend to a higher stage of existence, and the redemption of Israel cannot be fulfilled without this uplifting of the souls and their perfection. "This is a very great thing and a very great faith—that every one of Israel, by the faith in his heart, will hasten the coming of the redeemer . . . as it is said: 'Today if you obey Him'." Man must liberate himself because man is a microcosm,

* The sinister, evil, or demonic side of existence associated with the power of evil forces and the temptation to evil.—Ed.

and there is in him Pharaoh and Egypt; he is enslaving himself.

Just as there is a general redemption for "Knesset Israel," so there is also an individual redemption for each and every soul in Israel. "And though man himself knows his own crudeness and materiality, nevertheless he must always will with his whole heart to find a remedy for his soul and to liberate his material urges until he brings their roots to the upper world which is called 'the World of Freedom.' And that is why, 'When you buy a Hebrew slave, six years he shall work'—in virtues to make goodness overwhelm evil, until he reaches the seventh which is the World of Freedom." And again in a later age, with still greater clarity, "It is impossible that there shall be generality before there is individuality first. And what is individual redemption? That everyone shall destroy the evil in himself. And at that time there will be the will in every man to leave evil and destroy it from his heart—and this is the 'lower awakening.' God, blessed be His name, will help that there shall also be a 'higher awakening,' and all people will destroy the evil in their hearts and there will be individual redemption and later on there will be a general redemption, Amen." No man should say that we are unable to do such a great thing. Every one has his own part, and how great his capacity is he will not know until he makes an effort with all his might. Once, it is said, the holy "Yehudi" was walking in the field with his disciples and they met a peasant driving a cart full of hay. The cart happened to turn over and the peasant cried to the holy "Yehudi" and his disciples to help him set it straight and load the hay. They went to help him, but they did not feel sufficient strength. The peasant became furious and scolded them in Polish—"Moziesz ale nie checsz" they could help him, he claimed, but they did not want to. Then the holy "Yehudi" said to his disciples: "Do you hear what the peasant is saying? He is telling us that we can uplift the Holy Name (deliver the Shekina from exile) but we do not want to."

Pride, on the other hand, is the great obstacle, namely, if a man imagines that he has already done his duty in his spiritual action while in truth he has not even started with the essential thing—changing the goal of his life and his whole way of life. Once, it is said, the Rabbi of Lublin confidently expected that the full redemption would come that very year, but it did not. He explained that simple people had already accomplished the *teshuva* (turning) and so far as they were concerned, the redemption could have come, but the main obstacle came from the superior men, for it was hard for them to become humble due to the virtues in them, and therefore they could not accomplish the turning to God. But even the perfection of the individual is only a condition and not the goal. The most essential thing is that among these people a real comradeship should be created, and that all of them, the spiritual and the simple, those who can perceive the real meaning of redemption and those who cannot, should unite to work together for its sake.

The real evil in the exile is that the nation does not perceive the depth of its exile and its duty to overcome

210

it; if it would only perceive it, this would already be the beginning of the overcoming. Therefore, it may be said that the nation is in its own exile. "And God said to Moses, now you will see what I shall do unto Pharaoh, for he will send them with a strong hand and with a strong hand will he drive them away from his country." Because it became known that Israel was not worthy then of being delivered from Egypt. And it is known that the exile of Israel is their own exile, as they sink in sins and desires under the power of the sovereignty of the *kelipot,* so the *kelipa* and its hosts rule over them, and therefore the redemption is also the redeeming of themselves. When they shall be redeemed from the shells of darkness and subjugate the desire of their evil hearts and come out of the rule of the *kelipa,* then the power of those rulers will be broken and Israel will be saved from them. But Israel in Egypt, who did not know to redeem themselves, were not able to come out of the exile. Therefore, it was said in the name of Rabbi Yechiel Michal: "A slave who is compelled by his master to do all sorts of hard labor and who happens to have the opportunity to come out from his hand, does his master have to drive him away? Will he not run away as fast as he can just like a bird which is running away from a trap? And why did the Blessed Name cause Pharaoh to drive them away and not cause them to come out by themselves? The reason is that Moses understood that Israel was in its own exile and did not at all wish to come out of its exile in order to break the power of the sovereignty of the *kelipa* which was around them." Or in

211

the version of a later age: "The worst of the exile in Egypt was that they already endured everything." "And that is what is written: 'Who redeems you from under the endurances of Egypt,' your own endurance of the Egyptian tortures is meant." In the same way the redemption depends on the inner change in the nation, depends on its *teshuva*. If this turning, which, in the language of our day, Ahad Ha'am calls the revival of the hearts, has not yet happened, we are forbidden to delude ourselves by any external signs that it has already come. "In the days of the Zaddik Rabbi Mendel of Vitebsk" (who came to Palestine with three hundred Hasidim in the year 1773), "it happened in Jerusalem that a foolish man ascended the Mount of Olives and blew the Shofar without anybody seeing him. And among the masses of Israel the rumor spread that this was the Shofar blast which announces the coming of redemption. When the rumor reached the ears of the zaddik, he opened a window and looked out into the air of the world. And he said at once, 'Here is no renewal.'" Even the greatest effort will fail if the inner condition is missing. The people who have to take part in the decisive act are as if paralyzed from inside if the generation is not yet capable of making the decisive contribution to the redemption. Once, they say, the Maggid of Mezritsh demanded that the redemption come. He was asked from heaven: "Who is he that dares to hasten the end and what does he consider himself?" The Maggid answered, "Since I am the leading zaddik of this generation, it is my duty to contend for the redemption." The voice asked him:

"How can you prove that you are the leading zaddik of the generation?" The Maggid replied, "My holy community will come and witness that I am really the leading zaddik of the generation!" Then the voice from heaven said, "If so let your holy community rise up and give witness for you and then you will have proven that you are the zaddik of the generation." The Maggid went to his holy community and when they all sat before him asked them, "Is it true that I am the zaddik of my generation?" But nobody said "Yes" to this question. He asked them three times, and there was not a single person who would answer him.

The supreme type of exile and redemption, however, is the exile and redemption of the Shekina. Here, the other three types, the cosmic, the individual, and the national, find their sublimation and their perfection. In the tradition of the secret teaching, the exile of the Shekina is connected with the breaking of the ancient worlds, when the holy sparks have fallen into the shells, and also with the sin of Adam because of whom the souls of all people had to transmigrate from stage to stage. It is also connected with the guilt of Israel and its destiny, because the Shekina accompanies Israel into exile. The same thing is true of redemption. But the strongest tie is that which exists between the exile of Israel and its redemption, on the one hand, and the exile of the Shekina and its redemption, on the other hand. The picture which is known to us from the Bible, the picture of marriage and separation and a second marriage, is used for both types, but in the case of Knesset Israel it is the wife who is the cause of separa-

213

tion, while in the case of the Shekina, the separation comes of course not because of her, but because of the world, because of man, and mainly because of Israel. The two ideas come closer together when we consider that it is not right to aspire for individual redemption by itself, but for the redemption of all. This general redemption appears at times as the redemption of the Shekina and at times as the redemption of Israel. In this way, for instance, we find the two forms in two parables of the same zaddik, one of which refers to the redemption of the Shekina and the other one (as we know from the sayings of the zaddik) to the redemption of Knesset Israel.

Rabbi Bunam of Pshysha said:

"A king's son rebelled against his father and was banished from the sight of his face. After a time, the king was moved to pity his son's fate and bade him be sought out. It was long before one of the messengers found him, far from home. He was at a village inn, dancing barefoot and in a torn shirt in the midst of drunken peasants.

"The courtier bowed and said: 'Your father has sent me to ask you what you desire. Whatever it may be, he is prepared to grant your wish.'

"The prince began to weep. 'Oh,' said he, 'if only I had some warm clothing and a pair of stout shoes!'

"See," added Rabbi Bunan, "that is how we whine for the small needs of the hour and forget that the Divine Presence is in exile!"

And here is the other parable:

"Three men, two of them wise and one foolish, were

214

once put in a dungeon black as night, and every day food and eating utensils were lowered down to them. The darkness and the misery of imprisonment had deprived the fool of his last bit of sense, so that he no longer knew how to use the utensils he could not see. One of his companions showed him, but the next day he had forgotten again, and so his wise companion had to teach him continually.

"But the third prisoner sat in silence and did not bother about the fool. Once the second prisoner asked him why he never offered his help.

" 'Look!' said the other. 'You take infinite trouble and yet you never reach the goal, because every day destroys your work. But I sit here and try to think out how I can manage to bore a hole in the wall so that the light of the sun can enter, and all three of us can see everything.' " *

Because people do not follow this command, to aspire to the single thing which is the supreme principle, the Shekina asks of her husband that He Himself redeem her and come in contact with her again. God, blessed be His name, asks the Shekina: "Who is in exile if there are those who aspire to God and to unify you with Him and to uplift you to a full stature?" To this she answers in the words of the Bible: "I am your maid-servant Ruth. All the people have gone each his own way and nobody minds it, and nobody takes to his heart the exile of the Shekina in order to establish her and

---

* I have used here Olga Marx's translation of these two stories in Martin Buber, *Tales of the Hasidim: The Latter Masters,* op. cit., pp. 252 and 247 respectively.—Ed.

support her so that she is again together with her bridegroom. Since this is so, "you should bring your maid-servant under your wings because you are a redeemer. The redemption depends mainly on you, because nobody is concerned with redeeming me from exile."

Another story: When Rabbi Shalom of Belz's wife died, some time passed when suddenly he cried and wept much. Rabbi Samuel of Kaminka, his disciple, asked him: "What is new today that you were suddenly moved so much?" He answered him thus, "I was telling God, blessed be His name, 'Oh Master of the World, you know that if I could only lift up my spouse from the grave and bring her to life, there is no hardship in the world that I would not undertake to do so; the only difficulty is that it is not within my power to do so. But you have named yourself "husband" of Knesset Israel, "your husband and creator" and have named us "bride of your youth," and your bride of youth is prostrate on earth, and you have the power to lift her up and there is no obstruction or obstacle for you. How can you restrain yourself from lifting her up?' The Blessed Name answered me, 'If I should be satisfied with my spouse Knesset Israel as you were satisfied with your spouse, I would certainly lift her up.'" God's reply to the petitions for redemption is that Israel must *begin*. God is indeed the "redeemer," but the beginning must come from below, from man, from the nation.

Those zaddikim who have settled themselves in Eretz Israel, like Rabbi Menachem Mendel of Vitebsk, and those who have made the land the center of their life, like Rabbi Nachman of Bratzlav (who stayed in the land in the year 1798), have recognized that this beginning means bringing about the inner change of the nation by contact with Eretz Israel. The real conquest of the country depends on an inner change. But this change should not entail a separation from the world; the man who wills the redemption of the nation and the land must turn to face the world. "The whole holiness of Israel," says Rabbi Nachman, "is Eretz Israel. And when a man hallows and purifies himself, he conquers every time some part of Eretz Israel and works in repairing the road to Eretz Israel . . . The 'other side' is warring against him because he wants to conquer the holiness of Israel from their hands, and they accuse him, saying, 'You are robbers because you conquer a land which does not belong to you' . . . . Due to this, man must at times leave the study of the Torah and occupy himself with 'Derek Eretz' * . . . and in this way their accusation is refuted, and not only this, they themselves come and become converted and 'draw closer to the holiness.'" The life in the land also should not be based on separation, but we should accept the alien things in so far as they are close to us in soul and digest them in truth. "Eretz Israel," says Rabbi Nachman, "is . . . like the wholeness of the holy language . . . For the essence of the wholeness of the holy language lies in the fact that the good in 'foreign language' is also uplifted into it. That is why

* The way of the earth, i.e., the right way of life outside the revelation of the Torah.—Ed.

the tribes of Israel had to take part in Transjordan too, which has the nature of a 'foreign language,' and the tribes of Transjordan had to pass as pioneers before their brethren to conquer Eretz Israel, because the essence of the war and the victory is of the nature of 'foreign language,' in which good and evil are mixed, and by discarding the evil in it and uplifting the good in it into the holy language, we get the essence of the wholeness of the holy language which is the nature of the holiness of Eretz Israel."

Moses Hess said that we cannot foresee the consequences of Hasidism if it will be taken up by the national movement. This is also my opinion. Because here, in Hasidism, we have something close to us in time, and its off-shoots reach into our very age. Hasidism is a great revelation of spirit and life in which the nation appears to be connected by an inner tie with the world, with the soul, and with God. Only through such a contact will it be possible to guard Zionism against following the way of the nationalism of our age, which, by demolishing the bridges which connect it with the world, is destroying its own value and its right to exist.

# CHAPTER VIII

# THE PLACE OF HASIDISM IN THE HISTORY OF RELIGION

The task of ascertaining the place that Hasidism occupies in the history of religions does not include discovering its historical connections, the influences that worked on it, and the influences exercised by it, but showing which particular kind of religion has here found its historical form. We speak of the historical form of a kind of religion when it is not a question of personal thinking and personal experience alone, but of a communal movement growing out of several generations and of a communal life developing through several generations. To grasp the particular kind of religion that is represented by a historical manifestation, we must find out to which historical type this manifestation belongs, but after this we must also press forward to the limits of typology and identify the specific difference.

Our method is necessarily a comparative one, therefore, but in another sense than that with which we are familiar from the comparative history of religion. Of course, we too can begin by laying bare motifs in texts and rites that are common to them and to the texts and rites of other religious spheres, whether of a historical or of an ethnological-folkloristic character. But the lifting out of such motifs is not, for us, the task and event of our inquiry but its starting point. What we must do is to indicate in how many different ways in the history of religion the same motif is formed by different types, and, in addition to that, in how many different ways within the same type the same motif is formed by different manifestations, what significance the motif has taken on here and what there. And in this manner we must attain to a clear determination, first of the type and then of the individual historical manifestations. It is not the motif itself that is essential to us, but we want to know why the motif has been taken up into a certain order and what change has taken place in it through being taken up in this way.

For the critical elucidation of the task I begin with a tale through which one can show quite clearly how a certain theme is common to various religious realms, but through which we must at the same time recognize that the establishing of this common factor by itself means no great advance.

The story is told of Rabbi Aaron of Karlin, a favorite disciple of the Maggid of Mezritch, who died young. A fellow disciple on his way home from Mezritch came to Karlin about midnight and desired to greet his friend. He went at once to his house and knocked on the lighted window. "Who are you?" asked a voice from within, and, certain that Aaron would recognize him by his voice, he answered, "I." No reply came, and the door did not open even though he knocked again and again. Finally he cried, "Aaron, why do you not open to me?" Then he heard from within, "Who is it who presumes to say 'I,' as it is fitting for God alone to do!" He said in his heart, "I see then that I have not yet finished learning," and returned immediately to the Maggid.

We know this story, and indeed in a fuller version, from the literature of the Sufi sect of Islam, namely, from the first part of the collection of mystical parables "Masnawi" of the Persian poet Jalal-ud-din Rumi. Here no great Sufi is named, rather everything remains anonymous. A man knocks on the door of his friend. The latter asks, "Who is it?" He answers, "I." He sends him away. For a whole year the sorrow of separation burns in him, then he comes again and knocks once more. To the question of his friend, "Who is it?" he replies, "Thou." And at once the room is opened to him in which there is not room for two "I's," that of God (of the "friend") and that of man.

Doubtless this story does not originate with Rumi. In the view of Massignon and Paul Kraus his source is a saying of the mystical martyr al-Hallaj, quoted by Solami. There God rejects the faithful one who answers, "It is I," but receives him when he returns and now gives the answer, "No, it is thou, my Lord!" And in that moment his longing for God becomes God's longing for him.*

It is quite possible that the presence of the motif

---

* The sayings set forth by Nicholson in his commentary on the "Masnawi" are less analogous.

in Hasidism—in fragmentary form—is to be traced to Sufi influence, perhaps through Turkey in the Sabbatian era. So far as I know it cannot be proved. For us the question is unimportant here. For we do not have before us an inner link between Sufism and Hasidism alone that would testify to an especial closeness between them. We find parallels not only in the Indian Bhakti mysticism and in the Rhenish monastic mysticism of the Middle Ages, but also in a mystical system that in contrast to them all bears no theistic stamp, the Chinese Zen Buddhism with which we will be occupied further. There it is told how a monk from another Buddhist sect, following the advice of a Zen monk, becomes absorbed in inner contemplation in the latter's monastery. In the gray of morning he hears a flute playing, falls into ecstasy, runs to the cell of the Zen monk and knocks on the door. To the question, "Who is it?," he answers, "I." Then the other lets fly at him, "Why do you get drunk and snort away the whole night on the street?" The next day the man attains the "right attitude" and expresses it in these verses: "Now I no longer have an idle dream on my pillow, I let the fluteplayer blow in whatever way he wills." In the symbolic language of Zen this means that he no longer opposes the I to the Being but experiences the Unity.

We may regard this motif as one common to mysticism in general. In it the tendency to overcome the distinction between I and Thou in order to experience the unity has found a vivid expression. As regards typology, the comparison has not led us beyond the general realm.

We come much closer to the knowledge of what is peculiar to Hasidism when we compare some of its legends with legends of Zen, hence with just that sect, or more exactly one of that sect-group within the Mahayana, that held itself entirely at a distance from the theistic elements that had arisen in it. This proves that in comparing historical manifestations in the sphere of mysticism it is not always good to begin with a central religious content; it may be more fruitful to proceed from life itself, from the relation to concrete reality, and only finally to ask concerning the central content, which, of course, also exercises a certain influence on the realm of the concrete.

Zen (in Sanskrit *dhyana,* that is absorption, contemplation) is the name of one of the varieties of later Buddhism that gained a foothold in China in the sixth century and in Japan in the twelfth. Its most important characteristic is that it declines all direct utterance about transcendent matters. According to tradition, the Buddha himself refused to speak of the realm of the transcendent and gave as his reason that such talk is of no benefit in finding the path of salvation. The Zen school develops from this the teaching that one cannot even think of the absolute as such, much less express it. In a particular authoritative writing of the Mahayana, the Lankavatara Sutra, it says, "Concepts and judgments go together, they are unable to express the highest reality." This corresponds fully to the saying of Lao-tzu, "The Tao that one can express is not the

eternal Tao." In many formulations of Zen one can
mark the influence of the Taoist teaching that the
truth is above the opposites. All conceptual expression
subjects its object to the law of contradiction, it brings
it down to the plane of dialectic where it is possible
to oppose an antithesis to every thesis, and the absolute truth is thus transformed into a relative one. Therefore the Zen school even refuses to recognize the antithesis of concepts of classical Buddhism, that between
samsāra, the "stream" of incessant becoming, and
nirvāna, the running dry of the stream: in truth both
are one. "The highest truth," says an early Zen text,
"is not difficult, only it rejects choice," that is, the
rational compulsion to explain either a or non-a as
truth and not both at once.

The absolute, therefore, is not to be comprehended
through anything universal, but it can, indeed, be
comprehended from the sensible concrete, from something that we live. The Zen teacher tells the story that
when the Buddha wanted to preach the full teaching,
he held up a flower and silently smiled; only one in the
assembled throng understood him and likewise smiled,
his disciple Kassyapa. The Zen school traces its tradition back to Kassyapa who received the mystery from
the Buddha. The meaning of this tradition, accordingly,
cannot be that of handing down spiritual truths in conceptual speech. But also all established methods of
contemplation appear only as more or less questionable
expedients and not as the way to the attainment of the
truth; indeed, some even designate all contemplation
as sickness. When the disciple asks him about the

transcendent, the teacher shows the disciple, for example, his staff, as if to oppose the concrete to the universal. Or he lifts a finger. Or he breaks forth into the cry, famous in the history of the school, "Kwats!" Or, if he does speak, he speaks a verse. And at times he even gives the disciple a box on the ear in order to transport him at once into the reality where the mystery that is superior to all Yes and No is revealed to him, the mystery that can be transmitted in no other way than through its springing from the heart of the disciple under the influence of the teacher. "Everyone," it says, "should find the heart of the Buddha in his own heart." Not through turning away from reality but only through giving himself to it can man attain salvation. Zen cloisters are not places of contemplation for individuals, accordingly, but fellowship settlements of land-workers; work is the foundation of their life. Of the patriarch who founded this way of life in the eighth century it is told that when the monks besought him to expound the secret truth, he commanded them to work in the fields and said that he would speak to them after their return. When they came back, he went toward them, spread out his arms and pointed silently to them. Through the activity of the whole spiritual-corporeal being man attains intimate intercourse with concrete reality; in intimate intercourse with concrete reality one becomes capable of comprehending the truth, and in return the comprehending of truth leads to the highest concentration of action. From this comes the decisive influence that Zen has exercised on the warrior caste of the Samurai. The sword masters were accustomed, before they went into battle, to come to the great Zen teachers and to learn from them the highest concentration. There they recognized, as one of them says, that "those who cling to life are dead and those who defy death live."

I shall now compare some Hasidic tales with analogous tales of the Zen school.

It is told of Rabbi Shmelke of Nikolsburg that one of his disciples complained to him that "alien thoughts" disturbed him in prayer. The rabbi bid him go to another disciple, Rabbi Abraham Haim of Zloczov, who was at that time an innkeeper, and spend some time with him. For two weeks the disciple observed the customs of the landlord. He saw each day how he prayed and how he worked, and marked nothing especial in him. Only in the evening after all the guests had gone and in the early morning before they came, he did not know with what Rabbi Abraham Haim occupied himself. At last he dared to ask him about it. The latter said to him that in the evening he washed all the dishes, and as in the course of the night, dust settled on them, he washed them anew in the morning, but he was especially careful to see that they did not become rusty. When the disciple returned to Rabbi Shmelke and told him all this, he said, "Now you know what you need to know."

In the literature of Zen we find this motif in a more limited setting. A monk asks the Superior of his monastery, one of the great teachers of the ninth century, to reveal to him the mystery of the teaching. The teacher asks, "Have you already had your breakfast?" "Yes," he answers. "Then wash the dishes," the teacher says to him. And when he hears this, the disciple experiences the inner illumination.

In the Hasidic tale the symbolic character of the occurrence is stressed, whereas in the Zen tale it remains concealed, and in the literature the meaning of the utterance is discussed; but it can hardly be doubted that here too the washing of the dishes is a symbol of a spiritual activity. We would err, however, despite the explanation that is given in the Hasidic tale itself, if we understood the course of the matter as merely symbolic. It is also really meant that one should do whatever at one time or another one has to do (as here washing the dishes) with complete concentration, with the gathering together of all one's being, with whole intent and without turning one's eyes away from anything.

After the death of Rabbi Moshe of Kobryn, the Rabbi of Kotzk asked one of the disciples of the deceased what had been the most important things for his master. He answered, "Always just what he was engaged in at the moment." And the abbot of a Zen monastery is asked, "One of the first patriarchs has said, 'There is a word which, when understood, wipes out the sins of innumerable aeons.'—What is this word?" He answers, "Right under your nose!" The disciple asks again, "What does that mean?" "That is all that I can say to you," replies the teacher.

The two answers, the Hasidic and the Zen, are almost identical in essence: the key to truth is the next deed, and this key opens the door if one does what one has to do in such a way that the meaning of the action here finds its fulfillment.

The teacher, therefore, is the man who does all that he does sufficiently, and the core of his teaching is this, that he lets his disciple take part in his life and thus grasp the mystery of the action. Rabbi Mendel of Rymanov used to say that he had learned Torah from every limb of his teacher, Rabbi Elimelek. The same, only from the other side, is now expressed by the Zen teacher. When a disciple who serves him complains that he has not yet been introduced into the wisdom of the spirit, he answers, "From the day of your coming I have always instructed you in the wisdom of the spirit." "How so, master?" asks the disciple, and the teacher explains to him, "When you have brought me a cup of tea, have I not taken it from your hand? When you have bowed before me, have I not returned your greeting?" The disciple bows his head, and now the teacher elucidates further for him, "If you want to see, look straight into the thing; but if you seek to ponder over it, then you have already missed the goal!"

Thus truth in the world of man is not to be found as the content of knowledge, but only as human existence. One does not reflect upon it, one does not express it, one does not perceive it, but one lives it and receives it as life. That is expressed in Zen and in Hasidism in almost the same language. The "Song of Experiencing the Truth" of a Zen teacher of about the year 700 begins with the verse, "Have you never seen a man who is truth itself?" Hasidism says just the same when it applies the word of David, "And this is the

229

teaching of man" to the man who has himself become a completed teaching. Almost in the same language the holiest teaching is rejected both in the one place and the other when it is found in someone only as a content of his thought. According to the Hasidic view, it is dangerous "to know too much Hasidut," because one can come thereby to know more than one does, and one of the Zen teachers reproaches his disciple with this one failing, that he "has too much Zen"; "when one talks about Zen," he says, "it fills me with disgust."

Both in the one place and in the other silence is held in honor. And in both places what is intended is not refraining from all expression, but only renouncing all conceptual utterances about that which is not given to concepts. In both places there is singing, in both folk themes are brought into song and transformed into mystical ones. The Zen monk also paints, and his significance in the development of East Asiatic art is great. The Hasid cannot paint, but he dances. All this, song, painting and dance, means utterance and is understood as utterance. Silence is not the ultimate. "Learn to keep silent, in order that you may know how to speak," says a zaddik, and one of the Zen teachers says, "Talk is abuse, but silence it deceit. Beyond talk and silence there is a steep path." There is, however, one trait in addition that is common to Zen and Hasidism and that is very characteristic of both. In different variants in one place and the other one is told of secular conversation that the master conducts with his disciples, conversation that is disappointing to strange ears through its apparently complete superficiality while in truth word after word is full of hidden and weighty intention.

Both in Zen and in Hasidism the relation between teacher and disciple is central. Just as there is clearly no other people in whom the corporeal bond of the generations has attained such a significance as in China and Israel, so I know of no other religious movement that, to such an extent as Zen and Hasidism, has connected its view of the spirit with the idea of spiritual transplanting. In both, human truth paradoxically is not honored in the form of a possession but in that of a movement, not as a fire that one burns on the hearth, rather, to speak in the language of our time, as electric sparks that are ignited in the contact of the stream. In the one place and in the other the highest subject matter of legend is what passes between teacher and disciple. In Zen this is almost the only subject, whereas in Hasidism, which does not present itself in brotherhoods of isolated individuals, the community plays a great part; of course, it too is to a certain extent composed of potential disciples, of men who ask, seek explanation, listen, and time after time learn something that they had not intended to learn.

Yet this is also the point where the ways most obviously part. I should again like to quote a typical tale from both movements.

To a Zen teacher of the tenth century there comes a young man from a distant land. The teacher shuts the door in front of him. The youth knocks and is questioned as to his person and his desires. "I am able," he says, "to look to the ground of my existence, and I

231

desire to receive instruction." The teacher opens the door, gazes at the visitor and shuts it anew in his face. After a while the youth returns and the occurrence is repeated. The third time the stranger forces his way inside, the teacher seizes him by the chest and cries, "Speak!" When the latter hesitates, the teacher lets fly at him "You blockhead!" and thrusts him out. The door turns on its hinge, a foot of the disciple catches in it and breaks. He screams, and in that very moment he experiences the inner illumination. Later he founded a school of his own.

In Hasidism too we hear of the "severe" method, namely in the relation to the sinner who must turn back to God. But in the relation of the teacher to the questioning disciple it is not known here. Characteristic of this relation is the following incident. One of the disciples of Rabbi Bunam, Rabbi Enoch, tells how he longed for a whole year to enter the house of his teacher and talk with him. But each time he approached the house his courage deserted him. Once as he was walking about the field and weeping, the longing came over him with particular force and compelled him to run at once to the rabbi. The latter asked him, "Why do you weep?" Enoch answered, "Am I not a creature in the world and am created with eyes and heart and all limbs, and I do not know for what purpose I was created and what good I am in the world?" "Little fool," said Rabbi Bunam, "I too go about so. This evening you will dine with me."

We should err were we to think that the distinction here is essentially a psychological one, such as the distinction between pride and humility—although in Hasidism humility is counted one of the chief virtues, whereas in Zen it is not mentioned. The decisive distinction is of another kind. I shall illustrate it through showing how in both a widespread motif is elaborated, which we find first in an ancient Egyptian story, afterwards retold by Herodotus, and which reappears in much folk literature. It is the theme of the master thief. It is told of a Hasid of the Maggid of Koznitz that, following the latter's advice, he became a master thief and nonetheless remained an honest man; the tale recounts his cunning and his success. But the Hasidic tradition goes still further. Out of the mouth of some zaddikim we hear the jesting words in which the bold thief is set up as the model for the service of God since he stakes his life in his undertakings and what he once does not succeed in doing he tries again and again. The enterprise of the great thief appears here directly as symbol of concentration in the service of God. It is worth noting in this connection that at times the thief and the sucking child are juxtaposed: from these two beings, the immoral and the amoral, the highest quality, that of inner unity, can be learned. A wholly different symbolism of the life of a thief is to be found in Zen. A teacher of the end of the eleventh century tells in his sermon of an old master thief who undertakes to teach his son his art at the latter's request. He goes with him at night to the house of a rich man, breaks into the house together with him and commands him to climb into a great chest and to hide in it precious objects. When the son crouches down in the chest, the father pulls down the lid, bolts it, goes out of the room, alarms the members of the house, and leaves. The son must summon up all his wits to escape. Finally he appears in a fury before his father. The latter listens calmly to the whole story and then says, "Now you have learned the art." Thus the Zen teacher deals with his disciples. He makes nothing easy, he never interposes, he compels them to stake their lives and thus attain by themselves what one can only attain by oneself. We have seen that truth appears both to Hasidism and to Zen not as content and possession but as human existence and as movement between the generations; but this movement from existence to existence means in Hasidism transmission, in Zen stimulation.

This distinction, however, penetrates beyond the realm of the pedagogical, the relationship between the generations.

In a book ascribed to the first patriarch of Zen, Bodhidharma, we read, "If you wish to seek the Buddha, look into your own being, for this being is the Buddha himself." The message that he brought, when he came to China from the West about the year 520, is summed up in these verses: "Special transmission outside the writings, no clinging to words and signs, direct pointing to the soul of man, looking into one's own nature and attaining Buddhahood." This does not mean that the individual need only be concerned about his own salvation. In the fourfold vow that is repeated three times by the Zen teacher after every discourse, the last verse, to be sure, runs thus: "Inaccessible is the path of the Buddha, I vow to attain it," but the first verse says, "Innumerable are the sentient beings—I vow to save them all." And this saving again means, indeed, to help each look into his nature. The song of the late Zen teacher, a contemporary of the Baal-Shem-Tov, ends with the words, "This earth itself is the pure land of the lotus, and this body here is the body of the Buddha." The first of these two verses, to be sure, points to the importance of the intercourse wtih the concrete reality of the things, but the real path to the Absolute is seen only in the relation of man to himself. The historical Buddha, who, as is well known, became in the Mahayana a divine being that descends to earth, is here wholly pushed aside by this Buddha-nature which dwells in all souls and which every man is able to discover within him and to realize. Even the name Buddha is at times proscribed here because it diverts man from his personal task to historical memory—in contrast to the other Mahayana sects, which regard it as a way to salvation to repeat one of the names of the Buddha innumerable times. "He who utters the name of the Buddha," it says in a Zen writing, "should wash his mouth." In pictures by painters of the Zen school we see Bodhidharma as he tears up the holy scriptures and casts them from him. Another patriarch makes a fire in his oven with a wooden picture of the Buddha. There are even scruples against imagining the Buddha. The imagining of the Buddha is described as a chain that spiritual goldsmiths have hammered. "We," so it says further, "do not wear it." Zen is a religious manifestation that has severed itself from its historical antecedents. Buddhism, originally an historically-defined religion which was even transformed in Mahayana into a religion of revelation, becomes here a mysticism of the human person, a mysticism outside of history, no longer bound to any unique event.

It is entirely different with Hasidism. However much the Kabbalistic doctrine of emanations altered the view of the relation between God and the *world,* the view of the relation between God and the *human soul* remains essentially what it was. We do, indeed, hear in Hasidism ever again that God is the substance of our prayers, but we do not hear that He is our substance. The strength of God prepares our voice to speak the pure prayer, but the mouth that speaks is not divine. The elemental dialogue has not become a monologue, the dialogue of God and man has not become a conversation of man with his soul. It cannot become such because here from of old all existence of faith depends on the essential likeness of the divine leader and of the host led by Him, an essential likeness that could not change into an essential identity without raising doubt as to the unconditional superiority of this leadership. From here all fundamentals stem: the image of God, walking in His way, the holy order of the people.

Mysticism, it is true, here allows the soul of the individual who separates himself from society to feel the presence of God in flaming intimacy. But even in rapture the situation remains as it was; even the relationship of the most intimate reciprocity remains a relationship, the relation to a Being that cannot be

236

identified with our being remains unshaken. Even ecstasy cannot turn inward to such an extent that it finds full satisfaction and completion in inwardness. More than this, the detachment of the individual from society cannot take place in the realm of religion to such an extent that mysticism liberates itself from history. Even the most personal mysticism rests here in the shadow of the historical revelation. Never in the eyes of the soul has this God become to such an extent its God that He has ceased to be the God of Sinai. And certainly the true zaddik is a Torah, but he is it just because *the* Torah has become embodied in him. In the interpretation that I have mentioned of the verse of the Bible, "And this is the teaching of man," it says, "When man hallows himself in all his limbs and, spirit to spirit, cleaves to the Torah, he becomes himself a complete Torah." Even the most personal teaching arises out of the bond with the historical teaching. In Israel all religion is history, including mystical religion.

Here too an example may be cited. In Zen and still more clearly before it in Taoism, which, as we have said, had a great influence on Zen, we find at times the question whether we are not dreaming that we are alive. Chuang-tzu, the great Taoist poet and teacher, asks himself after he has dreamt that he was a butterfly, "Now I do not know: Was I then a man dreaming that he was a butterfly or am I now a butterfly dreaming that it is a man?" An answer is not given here; in Zen, in contrast, one answers such questions with a box on the ear that can be roughly translated by the cry, "Wake up!" Not so Hasidism. A zaddik is asked by his son, "If there are dead men who wander about in the World of Confusion and imagine that they are continuing their customary life, perhaps I too am dwelling in the World of Confusion?" The father replies to him, "If a man knows that there is a World of Confusion, then that is a sign to him that he does not dwell in the World of Confusion." A still more characteristic answer, however, was given by a zaddik who belonged to a generation close to our own to a disciple who asked how we can know that we are not living in the World of Confusion. The answer runs, "If a man in the house of prayer is called upon to participate in the reading of the Torah before the holy ark, that is a sign to him that he does not dwell in the World of Illusion." The Torah is the measure of reality.

After having established this fundamental distinction, we must consider afresh what seemed most clearly to us to be common to Zen and Hasidism, the positive relationship to the concrete. We have seen that in both the learning and developing man is directed to the things, to sensible being, to activity in the world. But the motive force thereto is fundamentally different in each. In Zen the intensive pointing to the concrete serves to divert the spirit directed to knowledge of the transcendent from discursive thought. Although aimed against the usual dialectics, the pointing is itself of a dialectical nature; it is not the things themselves that matter here, but their non-conceptual nature as symbol of the Absolute which is superior to all concepts. Not so in Hasidism. Here the things themselves are the object of religious concern, for they are the abode of the holy sparks that man shall raise up. The things are important here not as representations of non-conceptual truth but as the exile of divine being. By concerning himself with them in the right way man comes into contact with the destiny of divine being in the world and helps in the redemption. His activity with things is not like the activity of a Zen monk, something that only accompanies seeing into his own nature; rather it is permeated with independent religious meaning. The realism of Zen is dialectical, it means annulment; Hasidic realism is Messianic, it means fulfillment. As in its covenant with revelation it regards the past, so in its covenant with redemption it regards the future—both in contrast to Zen, for which unconditional reality is accorded only to the *moment* since in it is the possibility of inner illumination. Before the moment, thus understood, the dimension of time disappears. Hasidism, so far as I see, is the only mysticism in which *time* is hallowed.

Of all the manifestations of the history of religion Hasidism is that one in which two lines meet in full clarity, lines which it is usually assumed cannot meet by their very nature: the line of inner illumination and the line of revelation, that of the moment beyond time and that of historical time. Hasidism explodes the familiar view of mysticism. Faith and mysticism are not two worlds, although the tendency to become two independent worlds ever again wins the upper hand in them. Mysticism is the sphere on the borderland of faith, the sphere in which the soul draws breath between word and word.

239

CHAPTER IX

SUPPLEMENT:
CHRIST, HASIDISM, GNOSIS*

* This essay was first published in *Merkur* (Munich), Vol. VIII, No. 80 (October 1954) under the title "Christus, Chassidismus, Gnosis, Einige Bemerkungen" as a reply to Rudolf Pannwitz, "Der Chassidismus," *Merkur*, Vol. VIII, No. 79 (September 1954), pp. 810–830, a discussion of Buber's reconstruction of Hasidism. For Pannwitz's rejoinder to Buber's reply see *Merkur*, Vol. VIII, No. 81 (November 1954), "Mythos, Gnosis, Religion," pp. 1068–1071.—Ed.

In Rudolf Pannwitz's essay on Hasidism one finds, along with a penetrating understanding, some no less basic misunderstanding that ought in some measure to be clarified.

I　　Pannwitz believes that I am concerned with an issue between the Jewish and the Christian religion, and, indeed, "to the disadvantage of Christianity." No, I am not concerned with this, and in general I am not concerned with issues of this sort. Religions are mansions into which the spirit of man is fit in order that it might not break forth and burst open its world. Each of them has its origin in a particular revelation and its goal in the overcoming of all particularity. Each represents the universality of its mystery in myth and rite and thus reserves it for those who live in it. Therefore, to compare one religion with another, valuing and devaluing, is always an undertak-

ing contrary to being and sense: one's own temple
building which can be known from within the innermost shrine compared with the external aspect of the
alien temple as it offers itself to the attentive observer.
One may only compare the corresponding parts of
the buildings according to structure, function and connection with one another, honestly, but never valuing:
because their relationship to the ever invisible Sanctis-
simum is concealed. No, I am concerned now and I
am concerned in general with one thing, with the decisive issue within Judaism, within Christianity, and so
forth. Because it is everywhere the one thing essential,
I am allowed, bound and free as I am, to speak as I
speak.

The issue that I mean and in which I take part is that
between *devotio* and gnosis, that very gnosis which
Pannwitz rightly calls the "eternal that has a thousand
stages and forms."

In the factual existence, i.e., in the current actuality
of the lived life of a gnostic, as is also proclaimed in
the most spiritual of its utterances, gnosis means a
knowing relationship to the divine, knowing by means
of an apparently never wavering certainty of possessing
in oneself sufficient divinity. "Knowing" is a critical
word-formation; in my translation of the Bible the
spirits whispering secrets are called in faithful rendering of the Hebrew "the knowing." For the true gnostic
there is no unknowable; in high ages of gnosis he
draws the map of the seventh heaven and reports the
destinies of the Absolute from the primordial beginning; in other ages he plants the mystery in the incon-

243

testable psychic. All that, naturally, involves no commitment, unless it be that of liberating one's own self from all that impedes its pneumatic sovereignty. There stands over against it, the gnostic self, then, nothing with any higher right, nothing that can demand of it, visit it, redeem it: the gnostic redemption comes from the liberation of the world-soul in the self. In the manifold variants is hidden the same primal motif of the knowing majesty of the self in the all. It also has a love: which pretends to sleep with the universe.

*Devotio* means the unreduced service, practiced with the life of mortal hours, to the divine made present as over against one and ever again as over against, the divine with whom one can by no means presume, as Pannwitz remarks in censure, "be on intimate terms" with ("auf Du und Du stehen"), but to whom, in the language of the *vita humana* wholly turned toward Him in the everyday, one can say Thou (Du), that is, dare to stand toward him in free and serving over-against-ness. The great, inexhaustible presupposition is that he who so serves never and nowhere understands his self as *the* self—that unto the innermost depths of contemplation he still and ever again knows himself, rather, as *this* self over against the infinite Self, and relates to himself thus. More precisely yet: that in all service he holds in his hand his bodily death, his faithful mortality, as the most human of all presences and just thus, time after time, comes to meet the Eternal.

One asks this man: "What does it mean, to define God as over against you? That is, indeed, a crude anthropomorphism! Why, won't you tolerate it, then,

if God looks over your shoulder!" It should not be difficult to understand that this man only defines himself
and that he points to himself only practically and in
practice. His Lord may be on all sides of him—in that
this man serves Him He is over against him.

The gnostic cannot serve and does not want to be
able to. The man of *devotio,* of the "vow," does not
concern himself with the mysteries of his Lord, who is
his friend and who at one time and another shares
with him what he shares with him.

Gnosis is a great might in the history of the human
spirit. Of the might of *devotio* there is not much to discover on the surface of history; its highest trial of
strength is martyrdom—*devotio,* in fact, is what the
Romans called the self-sacrifice of generals for the sake
of victory. The issue between the two is joined for the
most on the plane of pure existence. Only at times, in
moments of a special danger, must it be joined in
words.

# II

Pannwitz reproaches me with "split-
ting" the "continuum of Christianity" because I separate that in it which is "gnosis and mystery" "not only
from the Jewish Christ but also from the *founder*
Christ."

That is an assertion that needs clarification before it
can be corrected. No one can split the continuum of a
religion. The continuum of a religion, in so far as one

considers it not in itself (with which I am not concerned), but in its human reality, is a historical one. That is, its inner dialectic, its arbitrations and settlements, transformations and returns, all belong essentially to it. Out of this vital dialectic the continuum originally forms and ever again establishes itself; receptions alternate with expulsions and schisms with reconcilations; the historical identity, the real continuum, maintains itself in and out of all of them, as the organism maintains itself in and out of the terrible inner battles that belong to its essential life just as long as it exists. But an observer who is also concerned in his observing about the continuance of the reality of faith, because he trembles for it as for the single bridge over the chasm of being, may not, for the sake of the historical consistency of the continuum, evade the full view of the primal antithesis between gnosis and *devotio* in its historical manifestations; for those hours and these have to do with each other. But, in particular, the observer who is "interested" to such an extent may not let this view be curtailed by the powerful undertakings of gnosis which readily efface the antithesis by lifting the historical-biographical out of its contingency into the spiritual.

Whom does Pannwitz mean by the "founder Christ" whom he knows how to distinguish from the "Jewish Christ"? This should mean the man who founded the Christian religion—by which it would be assumed that this man was Jesus of Nazareth. But Pannwitz evidently has no real human being in mind but the image sketched by the Johannine gnosis that since then has passed with a great part of Christendom as that of its founder. By the "Jewish Christ," in contrast, we undoubtedly must understand that remembered image held by those in whom the memory of their masters lives on, and just this image in so far as it is disclosed to us in the literary testimonies. When I have to deal with the content of faith and the manner of faith of Jesus, it is incumbent upon me to hold to this latter image and not to that other one; ultimately, indeed, to no image (even memory mythicizes, particularly memory that wishes to hand itself down), but to the one voice, recognizable ever anew, that speaks to my ear out of a series of undoubtedly genuine sayings: the contours of the speaker may be indistinct, but the voice is distinct enough. Significant to me in this speaker is what was clearly significant to him: persevering in immediacy with God, the great *devotio*. The message, as the bearer of which he spoke, was that of the "Kingdom of God" * that had "drawn near," that had approached quite near to the earthly, the Kingdom for the meeting with which the *devotio* of man should raise itself. This message does not speak, like the gnostic apocalyptics, of a "destruction of the aeon," but of its coming under the hand that extends itself to govern it.

Pannwitz knows of a "Christ," simply Christ, who has "taken in much gnosis." That is not Jesus of Nazareth. He does not, like the Gnostics, uncover the mysteries of the pleromas; he points to the door that stands

* "Heaven" is here no designation for an overworld but one of the names of God particularly familiar to the Israel of that time.

247

open in the Here, and he calls it *emuna*, trust, as the prophets called it. He who taught his followers to say "Our Father" could not give an account of himself as an "autarchic soul." He also has no share in the *kosmos atheos* * of the modern gnostic and just no place at all therein where he can lay his head.

What Pannwitz is concerned with and what he is not concerned with appears unmistakably in the sentence, "Christ produced" his sacrificial death "as a unique and conclusive embodiment of the Near Eastern sacred Easter drama." Out of the decision of the man to take on himself the suffering of which he has a presentiment and already senses and, if it must issue into the martyr's death, to make even this sacrifice too for "the many"— according to the prophetic proclamation for the serv-ants of God in all their "deaths" (Isaiah 53:9), † here the will to a "production" is made. I too know about the multiform mystery drama of divine dying and rising from the dead that had so great a share in the deifica-tion of the "risen one." But the real sacrifice of self is offered and not produced; it lives in the heart of the man ready to sacrifice himself, not in relation to a drama that awaits embodiment but in relation to the many for whom he wants to sacrifice himself. It is no *dromenon* transposed into life but the fulfilled *devotio*.

I hold the myth to be indispensable; yet I do not hold *it* to be central, but man and ever again man. Myth must authenticate itself in man and not man in

* Title of a book written by Rudolf Pannwitz in 1926.—Ed.
† Cf. my *Two Types of Faith,* p. 106 f., and my *The Prophetic Faith,* p. 231 ff.

248

myth. Yet I have not, Pannwitz to the contrary, uttered a negative valuation of Christianity even there where in it myth threatens to swallow man. I speak * of the salvation "which has come to the Gentiles through faith in Christ: they have found a God Who did not fail in times when their world collapsed, and further, One Who in times when they found themselves sunk under guilt granted atonement. This is something much greater than what an ancestral god or son of the gods would have been able to do for this late age." What is evil is not the mythicization of reality that brings the inexpressible to speech but the gnosticization of myth that tears it out of the historical-biographical ground in which it took root. Existential responsibility and myth bound to faith go together; existential responsibility and myth without faith do not go together.

But now Pannwitz reproaches me for having given Jesus "the guilt" of stepping out of the hiddenness of the servant of God. So next to the Foreword to my Hasidic chronicle-novel *For the Sake of Heaven,* † to

---

* *Two Types of Faith,* p. 132 f.

† In the Foreword to the new edition of his novel, Buber writes that he has been reproached with altering the figure of the hero, the Holy Yehudi, a zaddik of the school of Pshysha in the early nineteenth century, "under the sway of a 'Christianizing tendency.'" In reply Buber writes, "I have described no single trait of this man which does not exist in the tradition . . . Whatever in this book the Yehudi may have in common with Jesus of Nazareth derives not from a tendency but from a reality. It is the reality of the suffering 'servant of the Lord.' In my opinion the life of Jesus cannot be understood if one does not recognize the fact that he—as has been pointed out by Christian theologians too, especially by Albert Schweitzer—stood in the shadow of the concept of the 'servant of the Lord' as we find it in Deutero-Isaiah. But he emerged from the hid-

which he refers, let me quote an explanation written by me about two decades before [*]: "Whatever the appearance of Jesus means for the Gentile world (and its significance for the Gentile world remains for me the true seriousness of Western history), seen from the standpoint of Judaism he is the first in the series of men who, stepping out of the hiddenness of the servant of the Lord, the real 'Messianic mystery,' acknowledged their Messiahship in their souls and in their words. That this first one in the series was incomparably the purest, the most legitimate, the most endowed with real Messianic power—as I experience ever again when those personal words that ring true to me merge for me into a unity whose speaker becomes visible to me—alters nothing in the fact of this firstness; indeed it undoubtedly belongs just to it." All of this in no way bespeaks a "guilt." Like the other "servants" or arrows of God dwelling at one time or another "in the darkness of the quiver," Jesus too does not know without doubt whether he is destined to be taken out, to be shot; what is more, he does not even know without doubt whether he must not offer himself for that purpose if it should take place legitimately; and, according to Jewish teaching, to appear as "Messiah son of Joseph"

---

denness of the 'quiver' (Isaiah 49:2), while the Holy Yehudi remained within it. It is necessary to visualize the hand which first sharpens the arrow and then slips it into the darkness of the quiver, and the arrow which huddles in the darkness." Martin Buber, *For the Sake of Heaven,* trans. from German by Ludwig Lewisohn (New York: Meridian Books JP 1, 1953), p. xii f.—Ed.

[*] See above Section III—"Spinoza, Sabbatai Zvi, and the Baal-Shem."—Ed.

does indeed include martyrdom. If now, in an hour in which the question ascends from its depths,* he asks the men called "disciples," to whom he is directed for that purpose, who he is in their view (the gnostic, of course, never needs to do the like because for him, indeed, the self suffices) and receives the answer that he receives, then there happens as a result of it just what happens, the "pressing of the end," and it happens in highest innocence.

Like others before him, however, and out of a similar misunderstanding, Pannwitz seems to take exception, as a piece of arrogance, to a fact that I have expressly confessed,† namely, that I have "felt Jesus from my youth onwards as my great brother." So let me give the elucidation of this, the elucidation that, overestimating the understanding of my readers, I held superfluous: the Jews who are such through and through, from the original covenant, the "arch-Jews," among whom I dare to count myself, are "brothers" of Jesus. This too I have expressed before, twenty years earlier ‡: "that we Jews knew him (Jesus) from within, in the impulses and stirrings of his Jewish being, in a way that remains inaccessible to the peoples submissive to him."

* Cf. *Two Types of Faith*, p. 30 ff. The passage in the New Testament to which Buber refers is Mark 8:27–30.—Ed.
† *Two Types of Faith*, p. 12.
‡ Martin Buber, *Between Man and Man*, trans. by Ronald G. Smith (Beacon Paperback 1955), "Dialogue," p. 5 f.

**III**       If in the history of the founding of Christianity gnosis grafted its alien breed on to the natural plant *devotio,* in the religiousness of Judaism grown on the soil of the European diaspora an entirely different relationship between gnosis and *devotio* has existed.

Pannwitz, not without justification, sees in the Kabbala a great Jewish elaboration of gnosis; but his presentation suggests the view that Hasidism simply grew out of the Kabbala, that it was simply its entrance into the broad life of the people, hence that it was, so to speak, an applied gnosis. That, however, is not so.

In my first book about Hasidism (*The Tales of Rabbi Nachman,* 1907 \*) I wrote that it was the Kabbala become ethos. That is not, to be sure, an adequate description of the facts of the case, but an apt indication of them. One must really understand what that means when a gnosis becomes ethos: it is the true religious revolution that is only possible as the work of *devotio.* In order to find the way out of the crisis of the life of faith that had arisen through Sabbatianism, an inverted religious revolution borne along by delusion, in order from pronouncing sins holy, to find the new way, the way into the hallowing of the everyday, Hasidism

---

\* First published in English in 1956, trans. by Maurice Friedman (Horizon Press).—Ed.

turns back and takes up the Kabbala as gnostic * Sabbatianism had done. But the Hasidic movement takes
over from the Kabbala only what it needs for the theological foundation of an enthusiastic but not over-
exalted life in responsibility—responsibility of a single
one for the piece of world entrusted to him. Gnostic
*theologema* that are thus taken over are transformed,
their ground and their atmosphere are transformed
with them. From spiritualities enthroned in the unbinding, they become the core of authentications. The
pneuma has settled down in the blessings of a fervor
that fires with enthusiasm the service of the Creator
practiced in relation to the creature. Therefore, everything has become different. In the place of esoterically
regulated meditations has stepped the unprescribable
endowing of each action with strength of intention,
arising ever again from the moment. Not in the seclusion of the ascetics and schools of ascetics does the holy
now appear, but in the joy in one another of the masters
and their communities. And—what was unthinkable in
the circles of the old Kabbala, the "simple man" is held
in honor, that is, the man of the original *devotio*, the
man by nature at one with himself who lacks the secret
knowing as well as the rabbinical knowledge, but can
do without both because united he lives the united
service. Where the mystic vortex circled, now stretches
the way of man.

* Pannwitz's designation "Ahrimanic naturalism" can only be
explained as an unfamiliarity with the genuine gnostic theology
of Sabbatianism that the researches of Gershom Scholem have
disclosed to us.

In Hasidism *devotio* has absorbed and overcome gnosis. This must happen ever again if the bridge over the chasm of being is not to fall in.